Education in Pacific Island States
Reflections on the Failure of 'Grand Remedies'

About the Series

Pacific Islands Policy examines critical issues, problems, and opportunities that are relevant to the Pacific Islands region. The series is intended to influence the policy process, affect how people understand a range of contemporary Pacific issues, and help fashion solutions. A central aim of the series is to encourage scholarly analysis of economic, political, social, and cultural issues in a manner that will advance common understanding of current challenges and policy responses.

Pacific Islands Policy co-editors and editorial-board members are all affiliated with or on the staff of the Pacific Islands Development Program (PIDP) at the East-West Center.

Series Co-Editors

Robert C. Kiste
Adjunct Senior Fellow, PIDP
Professor Emeritus, University of Hawai'i

Gerard A. Finin
Resident Co-Director, PIDP

Series Copy Editor

Susan E. Arritt

Editorial Board

Sitiveni Halapua
Nonresident Co-Director, PIDP

Tarcisius Kabutaulaka
Adjunct Fellow, PIDP
Associate Professor of Pacific Islands Studies, University of Hawai'i

Geoffrey M. White
Adjunct Senior Fellow, PIDP
Professor of Anthropology, University of Hawai'i

Pacific Islands Policy
ISSUE 8

Education in Pacific Island States
Reflections on the Failure of 'Grand Remedies'

VICTOR LEVINE

THE EAST-WEST CENTER promotes better relations and understanding among the people and nations of the United States, Asia, and the Pacific through cooperative study, research, and dialogue. Established by the US Congress in 1960, the Center serves as a resource for information and analysis on critical issues of common concern, bringing people together to exchange views, build expertise, and develop policy options.

THE PACIFIC ISLANDS DEVELOPMENT PROGRAM (PIDP) was established in 1980 as the research and training arm for the Pacific Islands Conference of Leaders—a forum through which heads of government discuss critical policy issues with a wide range of interested countries, donors, nongovernmental organizations, and private sector representatives. PIDP activities are designed to assist Pacific Island leaders in advancing their collective efforts to achieve and sustain equitable social and economic development. As a regional organization working across the Pacific, the PIDP supports five major activity areas: (1) Secretariat of the Pacific Islands Conference of Leaders, (2) Policy Research, (3) Education and Training, (4) Secretariat of the United States/Pacific Island Nations Joint Commercial Commission, and (5) Pacific Islands Report (pireport.org). In support of the East-West Center's mission to help build a peaceful and prosperous Asia Pacific community, the PIDP serves as a catalyst for development and a link between the Pacific, the United States, and other countries.

Published by the East-West Center

A PDF file and information about this publication can be found on the East-West Center website. To obtain print copies, please contact

Publication Sales Office
East-West Center
1601 East-West Road
Honolulu, Hawai'i 96848-1601 USA

Tel: 808.944.7145
Fax: 808.944.7376
EWCBooks@EastWestCenter.org
EastWestCenter.org/pacificislandspolicy

ISSN 1933-1223 (print) and 1933-172X (electronic)
ISBN 978-0-86638-229-8 (print) and 978-0-86638-230-4 (electronic)

© East-West Center 2013

Table of Contents

Executive Summary	1
Preface	3
Methodology and data sources	4
The risk of generalizations	4
The State of Education: Evidence	7
Access	7
Quality	8
Equity	10
Efficiency	11
Sustainability	12
Assessment and accountability	13
Hypotheses About Underlying Causes	15
Inadequate funding	15
Do Pacific Islanders value education?	16
Mismatch with Pacific culture	17
Lack of technical capacity	18
Education as a source of public employment	18
Weak governance	21
No incentives to improve efficiency	23
Weak civil society	25

History of "Grand Remedies"	26
Large infusions of donor funding	26
Technical assistance, analysis, and reports	26
National education plans	27
Regional donor projects	28
Regional meetings and ministerial initiatives	30
Capacity building	30
Education management information systems	32
Donors	33
Migration	37
International Evidence on What Works	39
Spending	39
Teacher credentials	40
Staffing and class size	41
Flexible labor markets	42
Teacher attrition	42
Accountability and incentives	43
Supply-side financing and government service delivery	43
High subsidies for tertiary students	44
Education and economic growth	44
Countable inputs as proxy quality/outcome indicators	44
Options for Reform	46
Incentives	48
Feasibility	49
Managing the process	50
References	55
The Author	61

Abbreviations

ADB	Asian Development Bank
AusAID	Australian Agency for International Development
BELS	Basic Education and Literacy Support
EFA	Education for All
EMIS	education management information systems
FBEAP	Forum Basic Education Action Plan
FEdMM	Forum of Education Ministers Meetings
MDG	Millennium Development Goals
ODA	official development assistance
OECD	Organisation for Economic Co-operation and Development
PIC	Pacific Island country
PICL	Pacific Islands Conference of Leaders
PIFS	Pacific Islands Forum Secretariat
PILL	Pacific Islands Literacy Levels
PREL	Pacific Resources for Education and Learning
PRIDE	Pacific Regional Initiatives for the Delivery of Basic Education
SIDS	small-island developing states
SPBEA	South Pacific Board of Educational Assessment
UNESCO	United Nations Educational, Scientific and Cultural Organization

Executive Summary

In this report on education in the Pacific Islands, Victor Levine uses an informal and personal approach. He combines information from online data sources, government and donor reports, the popular press, and his own experience to review the state of education, hypotheses about the underlying causes of declining standards in Pacific Island education, "grand remedies" that have been attempted, the role and incentives of donors, and the impact and implications of migration. Levine then views the history of interventions in the context of empirical evidence regarding what seems to work and what does not work in education, comparing policy and practice in Pacific Island countries (PICs) to new empirical evidence.

For most of his professional career, Levine acknowledges, he has been a party to ineffective "grand remedies" that used economic analyses and models to generate technical reports that had little real impact. Past attempts at technical solutions have been ineffective, he says, because they do not address the core problems undermining education-service delivery. In fact, these attempts may have been counterproductive in that they obscured the basic problems and provided perverse incentives.

Levine poses a fundamental question: Can Pacific Island states realistically aspire to ever provide decent education to their children? There are strong incentives on the part of politicians, national education ministries, and international donor organizations to continue using the same ineffective approaches of the past, albeit with new acronyms and titles—like the proverbial "old wine in a new bottle." With measured optimism, however, Levine contends that in individual countries, if sufficient political will and leadership exist, meaningful reform may be possible.

Levine suggests some options that leaders might want to consider for initiating a reform process. He maintains that learning occurs in the classroom and that the teacher is the single most important factor affecting student outcomes. Many of the "grand remedies" have not been effective because they are remote from the basic problem of ineffective classroom teaching. Therefore, Levine asserts, the most essential change is to move from a culture where the education system is used to create jobs to one where the core objective is student learning. Individuals who demonstrate that they are able to help children learn should be hired and retained as teachers; those who do not perform should be replaced. This would require a fundamental shift in assessment, moving from counting inputs to actually measuring annual increases in student performance—"value added." If employment were contingent on productivity, other problems such as teacher attendance, motivation, principal supervision, and more would take care of themselves.

Levine argues against high-profile reform initiatives and suggests that the starting point is for a national leader to commission an objective and independent collection and analysis of the facts, using analysts from central ministries—outside the national or donor education establishments. He suggests that, to be effective, the process should be done in-house rather than by a donor or regional organization, and it should avoid presenting recommendations for reform. Once objective data are available and presented in accessible, nontechnical language, it might then be possible to initiate an internal dialogue regarding the need and options for change. The same information could provide a basis for developing national consensus and popular support for change.

The fundamental issues are straightforward, says Levine, and complex technical documents, regional conferences, and complex national plans actually obscure the basic problems and thereby constitute impediments to change.

Preface

In the first issue of Pacific Islands Policy, published in 2006, Francis X. Hezel, SJ, discusses the complex issue of whether two small Micronesian economies can realistically aspire to ever become economically self-sufficient and free of aid dependency. He combines data with personal musings and traces the changes in the context of development theory and dogma with changes in his own personal perceptions and experiences.

This report has a far less ambitious goal. Rather than address complex issues of macroeconomic models, growth theory, comparative advantage, and the like, I pose a far simpler question: Can Pacific Island states realistically aspire to ever provide decent education for their children? Like Hezel, I will share my personal experiences, musings, and the evolution of my views during almost four decades of international development experience—from the perspectives of a returned Peace Corps volunteer and young graduate student filled with enthusiasm for technical solutions, to those of an older practitioner who has come to realize and reluctantly accept that the binding constraints to providing decent education are not technical, and that over-reliance on so-called technical remedies may, in fact, be part of the problem.

This issue of Pacific Islands Policy was envisioned as a catalyst to stimulate discussion among the Pacific Islands Conference of Leaders (PICL), which is comprised of the 20 heads of government from the Pacific Islands region. I have limited my discussion and "evidence" to these 20 states, although the issues would apply to most developing countries in the region. Most of the issues raised do not apply to the four high-income PICL states; however, problems in developing neighbor states do impact some of these high-income states, particularly through migration.

Given that the primary intended audience is state leaders, this report avoids detailed discussion of technical education issues and focuses on the broader issues of governance and public-service delivery. To that end, this report differs substantially from a typical technical report; there are no tables or graphs, nor are the methodology and data sources traditional. Following Hezel's approach, my objective is to present an informal, personalized narrative—more insights and observations than cold facts.

Methodology and data sources
I have drawn on a combination of four sources of evidence:

- **Quantitative data.** These are presented, where available, but used judiciously. I obtained these data from online databanks managed by international organizations.
- **Official government and donor reports.** The advantage of drawing from these reports is that quantitative data presented are generally reliable. The disadvantage is that they often paint a biased and overly optimistic picture. Also, factual reliability can mask reality; it is quite easy to select the statistics that tell the best story.
- **The popular press.** The danger inherent in citing the popular press is that information it reports is sometimes unreliable. Also, press reports can reflect a political bias or seek a sensational headline; many of the sources I cite are editorials. However, the popular press often reflects the true concerns of the general public.
- **Personal experience and musings.** In this report I refer to situations and experiences I have encountered in almost forty years of working in education and development. In these personal accounts, I have avoided identifying specific countries so as not to violate professional confidentiality.

Following Hezel's lead, I have focused on identifying issues and have avoided suggesting remedies. As this report unfolds, it will become clear that, in my opinion, part of the problem with education in the Pacific has been excessive reliance on the advice of external technical experts. I propose some strategies and options for national leaders to initiate a process of identifying causes and remedies.

The risk of generalizations
The diversity of the Pacific region is well documented; in addition to the major differences between Melanesia, Polynesia, and Micronesia, considerable differences exist between countries within each region. Also, there are significant differences between districts and islands within countries, and certainly between urban centers and remote outer islands.

Pacific Island states also differ in terms of language, culture, and colonial legacy—each of which are reflected in the structure of each state's "inherited" education system. And they differ in their patterns of internal and external migration. It is therefore risky to make generalizations about Pacific Islanders. The 20 PICL states also differ substantially in size, per capita income, migration patterns, and education indicators. Fourteen of the states are recipients of official development assistance (ODA); 13 participated in the most recent regional education project, Pacific Regional Initiatives for the Delivery of Basic Education (PRIDE). Clearly, many points presented in this paper do not apply to the few high-income states in this group.

Despite important differences, there are many shared characteristics and common problems. Most PICL states have dispersed populations, long distances between islands, and transportation and infrastructure constraints; many are also highly dependent on external donor assistance. There is general agreement that many countries do face common problems. Reviewing a recent study of the region, the secretary general of the Pacific Islands Forum Secretariat (PIFS), Tuiloma Neroni Slade, noted that "despite the substantial differences in social, historical, demographic and economic contexts, the 14 countries under review are experiencing many of the same challenges" (PIFS 2009a).

Education in Pacific Island States
Reflections on the Failure of 'Grand Remedies'

The State of Education: Evidence

Now that more than fifteen years have elapsed since the 1996 Pacific Islands Literacy Levels (PILL) results documented the alarming low levels of student performance in the region, it is useful to take stock and ask, "Is the glass half empty or half full?"

Before highlighting the problems that exist in many PICs, it is important to emphasize that in each country there are a number of excellent, high-performing schools. Some of these schools are among the best anywhere, and alumni include heads of state, governors, business leaders, academics, and senior government officials. Many of these high-performing schools are privately owned, others are run by churches, and some are government-owned public schools. The discussion that follows focuses on the problems that are common in many, but not all, developing PICs.

Access

In many PICs there has been substantial progress in improving primary-education access and gender equity. Many countries have reduced or eliminated school fees for basic education; others are developing plans to do so. While basically positive, the access picture is mixed. The Asian Development Bank's latest monitoring report on the Asia Pacific Millennium Development Goals (MDG) indicates that, as a group, the Pacific Islands are regressing or showing no progress on primary enrollment and completion (ADB 2010a, Table I-1). Five of the PICL countries are regressing on at least one of the MDG education indicators (Table I-2), and three PICLs have seen a drop in net primary enrollment ratios (Table A-3). Much of the progress was experienced in the 1990s; more recently, in some countries, momentum seems to be lost. The picture is even less sanguine if one defines basic education as covering both primary and lower secondary. In many countries, "enrollments at secondary levels of education have stagnated" (World Bank 2006).

A recent report by the Australian Agency for International Development (AusAID) provides an assessment of the status of 14 PICL countries in meeting MDG 2 (universal primary education). Nine of the 14 countries were rated as being either "off-track" or "of concern" in meeting this goal (analysis of AusAID 2009, Table 3). Moreover, even when enrollment is increasing, there remain problems in attendance.

> **Around 40 percent of school children in Pacific Island countries do not complete primary school, and only 20 percent graduate from secondary school.**

There have been isolated instances where school-fee reforms have not been successful and policies have been reversed (*National* 2007). In general, fee income lost to schools has been offset by increased grant allocations, often funded by donor agencies. This raises some concern about the long-term sustainability of the grants system and sidesteps the more fundamental question of whether the need for school fees reflects an unbalanced allocation of resources to salaries, at the expense of other critical inputs. This issue is treated in more detail in section two, within the discussion of workfare.

While there has been progress in enrollment, many students are still out of school or fail to complete primary school. It is estimated that about one million school-aged children around the Pacific do not go to school at all, around 40 percent of school children in PICs do not complete primary school, and only 20 percent graduate from secondary school (Young 2011).

Quality

In many countries the quality of education has been stagnant or has declined. Comparative data on quality are limited; "there are shortcomings in the available data such as lack of up-to-date assessment data, inconsistencies, and reliability problems" (PIFS 2006, 4). AusAID says, "Tracking the quality of education is complicated by a lack of objective and consistent measures of how much children learn at school. Data from national examinations are often undermined by the practice of adjusting 'brackets' to meet pass rate targets and by cheating. International comparative tests are more reliable but cost limits them to small sample studies" (AusAID 2007). To a large extent, the lack of data reflects disinclination by PIC governments to release information and an aversion to comparisons between countries.

Where data do exist, they paint a distressing picture. "In many countries student performance on examinations indicates low levels of literacy and numeracy. For example, in English literacy tests administered in the mid1990s, over 40 percent of students in several countries were found to be 'at risk' in Year 4 and by Year 6 the situation was even worse" (PIFS 2006, 5).

There is growing recognition that the international focus on improving access while ignoring quality has not been effective. "The focus should be on improving learning achievements, as completing school will not necessarily provide children with the basic skills for poverty reduction" (AusAID 2007, 1). For example, a 2006–2007 household survey in one PIC found that "only 28.1% of those who complete primary school are literate…and less than half of those who complete secondary school are literate" (ASPEW 2007, 19). Students are being pushed through the education system at high costs, with few tangible benefits.

The crisis in quality features prominently in the regional press and in international reports:

Here's the problem: The [country] has an admittedly lousy public elementary and high school education system (*Marshall Islands Journal* 2001).

[It is] a flop education system, which lacks proper planning by policy makers (*Solomon Star* 2006).

There is clearly also a crisis of quality in our schools (ASPEW 2007, 19).

All countries continue to experience major gaps in terms of quality of education. Although very little reliable regional data exists, countries and technical agencies feel that quality has stagnated or even regressed. There is little evidence to indicate that quality is improving (PIFS 2009, 61).

As attention turns to quality issues, there is an increasing realization that quality issues are much more difficult to address:

While there has been considerable progress towards equitable access to education in recent years, supporting quality learning outcomes remains a challenge (AusAID 2010, 8).

Equity

It is also difficult to obtain data on equity in most PICs. Many PICs are experiencing high levels of urban migration. Urban-rural income differentials tend to be pronounced as new immigrants to urban areas often face unemployment and low wages, further compounding income inequality. While data on income distribution in PICs are limited, one source provides data on six PICs (circa 1990–2000); for these countries, income inequality is high (Abbott and Pollard 2004, Table 9).

In terms of educational equity, income inequality is particularly problematic if elites are able to manipulate the system to gain an unfair share of public finance. At the primary-school level, the elimination of school fees is pro-poor; statistics on gender equity have also improved. At the secondary level, equitable access is more problematic: "Equity issues have appeared, particularly in secondary education as poorer children dropped out or were squeezed out of the education system" (World Bank 2007, i).

> **Income inequality is particularly problematic if elites are able to manipulate the system to gain an unfair share of public finance.**

There are marked income-related differences at the secondary level. This is attributed to a combination of factors: low-income students are less likely to attend school and when they do attend, school quality is lower; as a result of low-quality primary education, many students fail to reach the required cut-off grade to enter public secondary schools; and, unlike more affluent families, students from low-income families cannot afford private secondary education (World Bank 2006).

Even if low-income students are able to complete secondary school, they are less likely to have grades that allow them to enter tertiary education. Equity problems in access are compounded by systematic income-related differences in student performance. For students who do manage to enter secondary school, there are pronounced differences in achievement, related to family socioeconomic status. This issue is not limited to the Pacific, but is a well-documented global phenomenon (World Bank 2011a).

In two PICs, I was able to construct cohort examination data, following the same children from primary through secondary school. Exam results at the end of secondary school were almost perfectly predicted by students' performance at the end of primary school. Differences in primary outcomes cascade through the system. Low-quality primary education almost always precludes gaining access to highly subsidized post-secondary education.

The greatest source of inequality relates to public expenditure on postsecondary education. In most PICs, there is a major imbalance in the use of public funds between basic and post-secondary education. As is the case worldwide, children from wealthier households have substantially better prospects of attending tertiary education. In some PICs, political and other elites appear to have unfair advantage in accessing publicly funded scholarships for study overseas. This is compounded by the policies and behavior of bilateral donor agencies which use scholarships to promote study in their own national universities. Even donor countries such as Australia, which applies progressive cost-sharing and cost-recovery at home, do not promote these reforms in recipient countries. New Zealand's education aid has been criticized as "skewed toward giving islanders tertiary education in New Zealand" (PINA Nius Online 2001). While recent policies have clearly been focused on reducing or eliminating school fees for basic education, it is still likely that, overall, education finance is regressive. Additional data and analysis are needed before one can make an informed judgment.

My own observation, based on work in two PICs, is that policymakers prefer not to know the equity implications of education finance policies. In both instances, although donor funding was available to support a benefit-incidence analysis, government officials preferred not to have these analyses done.

Efficiency

There is wide consensus that expenditure on public services in the Pacific is inefficient. A recent AusAID review observed that "Despite large investments in service delivery, public spending by Pacific governments is generally not leading to better development outcomes" (AusAID 2009, 1).

Even when compared to other small-island developing states (SIDS), which may face similar constraints, PICs do poorly in terms of efficiency.

> Pacific countries have, in general, fared less well than other SIDS during recent decades. Although these countries have had health and education expenditures at levels similar to other countries, health and education outcomes have shown little improvement during the last decade and some have even deteriorated (Feeny and Rogers 2008, 527).

Criticism of efficiency is not only voiced by donor agencies but is also acknowledged by political leaders and senior civil servants. A recent Asian Development Bank (ADB) study reported on interviews with five former Micronesian heads of state: "There was unanimous agreement among the presidents on the need to strengthen performance and raise productivity in the civil service and across the public sector" (Duncan 2010, 128).

Some of the presidents' comments about civil servants were surprisingly frank:

> People don't work, but they still get paid. Why they come to work is to get paid (Duncan 2010, 128).

> Taking five people to do a job that maybe one or two people can do, or putting off work that could be done today until tomorrow or getting paid for 8 hours when you are only working 5 or 6 hours (Duncan 2010, 129).

> We do not always hire the most qualified people. Nepotism is still an issue everywhere (Duncan 2010, 132).

> Ministers hire their wives, nephews, and nieces to government jobs (Duncan 2010, 130).

Efficiency problems are even acknowledged by some senior education officials, although criticism is often leveled at other levels of the system. One education secretary observed that "management inefficiencies and lack of good governance contribute to the problems confronting education in provinces" (*National* 2004).

Compared to countries in other regions with similar economic conditions, PICs spend considerably more per pupil on education and attain markedly poorer results.

> Corruption and inefficiency by successive governments in the countries of the region have left a grim toll in poor education performance marked by low school attendance and survival rates, high dropout and illiteracy rates, and substandard education quality (ASPEW 2007, 1).

In summary, low efficiency is one of the key problems in the region. High expenditure yields unacceptably poor academic results; students are not prepared to take up the curriculum in the next level of the system. Graduates of higher levels do not have the skills required to compete in a global economy. However, many may join the public sector, often as teachers, where skills and competency may not be a prerequisite for employment.

Sustainability

Sustainability is directly linked to issues of efficiency. In many PICs the provision of education services is overly dependent on external donor assistance. As

Hezel has pointed out, in many cases the costs of service delivery have been escalated by external donor support for services which, in some countries, are unnecessary and inappropriate. Whether intentional or not, many donor policies mitigate against financial sustainability and increase dependency.

Assessment and accountability

Assessment has been the Achilles' heel of most education systems in the Pacific region. This weakness impacts on quality and efficiency as key information critical to improving systemic performance, setting standards and benchmarks, and implementing accountability and incentive systems are lacking. The limited data that do exist are often not made public. One is led to the conclusion that politicians and leaders prefer not to know. Or, certainly, they don't want this information to be available publicly.

The problem is not by any means limited to the education sector; international statistical databases simply do not include many indicators for most PICs. Data and statistics are inadequate across all sectors:

> The limitation on quality and types of statistics across the Pacific inhibits effective monitoring and reporting, socioeconomic analysis, informed policymaking, and effective planning (ADB 2007, 1).

> In general, Pacific developing member countries fall short in generating the data required for results-based management and monitoring of national poverty-reduction strategies, national development plans, and progress toward the Millennium Development Goals (ADB 2007, 2).

Due to data deficits in small states, the World Bank prepared a special supplement to its 2011 publication of world development indicators; this included ten measures of participation in education (World Bank 2011a, Table 5). Compared to other small states, PICs were a third more likely to be missing data on education, with an average response rate of 4.7 versus 7.8 for other small states. It appears that information deficits are not due to the small size of governments or constraints in technical staff; for whatever reasons, PICs are reluctant to collect and share information.

The problem is not simply lack of data; to the extent that data do exist, they are underutilized for policy and planning, for assessing trends, and of greatest importance, for establishing

> **The problem is not simply lack of data; it is that data are underutilized for policy and planning.**

an accountability framework linked to genuine incentives to improve quality and efficiency. Therefore, initiatives to generate more data and information are unlikely to have any impact unless there is a commitment to transparent use of information.

Eight PICL members do participate in the South Pacific Board of Educational Assessment (SPBEA) secondary examinations system. While extremely useful for facilitating common accreditation, these exams cover only secondary education and are not regularly used to compare the efficiency of secondary education in participating countries. It should be noted that it took 16 years of discussion and negotiation to reach agreement on the exams (SPBEA 2011).

I have worked on educational projects in several PICs where education authorities claimed that they did not have SPBEA data; the data were held by the SPBEA which (as reported by national officials) was reluctant to share information. The SPBEA takes the position that it must keep this information confidential, as it is the "property" of the participating country. In my experience, whatever the actual causes of these obstacles, the data are simply not available for policy analysis.

At the primary-school level, the SPBEA conducts the Pacific Islands Literacy Levels (PILL) assessment at Years 4 and 6. Here again, while there are confidential reports to authorities in participating countries, the data are generally not disseminated to the public or to other stakeholders. Extensive searches of academic and donor databases include almost no references to PILL; the information is simply obscured. In the few instances where there is reference to PILL, comparative results and trends are simply not reported. A common explanation is that "the results cannot be discussed in detail in this article, because they remain national property" (Withers nd, 4). As a recent World Bank report on improving delivery of social services noted, "country level data is held confidentially for all but a handful of Pacific countries" (World Bank 2006, 30).

> **The data are generally not disseminated to the public or to other stakeholders.**

In June 2010, AusAID funded an SPBEA project to expand collection of baseline literacy and numeracy assessment in PICs. Baseline assessments for Years 4 and 6 are planned in eight PICL states. Data collection has been completed in five of the eight states. In four states, this represents a second round of data collection (SPC 2011) which, in principle, provides a basis for assessing trends over time. One of the stated objectives of the initiative is to "report and disseminate the results of assessments to policy makers" (SPBEA 2011). It is not clear whether there is a policy on wider dissemination of findings. Failure to disseminate results was recently identified as an issue in an SPBEA press release. According to Ana Raivoce, SPBEA director, "The failure to disseminate the reports of baseline achievements in literacy and numeracy in Forum island countries remains one of the challenges facing education authorities in the region" (PIFS 2010).

Pacific Resources for Education and Learning (PREL) works extensively with the state educational agencies of the US-affiliated Pacific Islands. The organization indicated that, in response to specific requests, some education agencies do provide aggregate and/or raw data for analysis. It is PREL's perception that capacity in data analysis varies across the region, but is improving.

The bottom line is that assessment systems are extremely weak, despite efforts to strengthen them. While these data are useful in targeting remediation to individual students, they are underutilized in systemic reform. A recent World Bank report comments on "the paucity of reliable data to analyze the strengths and weaknesses in the system. In the instances where data do exist, weak analysis and underutilization of the data result in unrealized potential from a policy making perspective" (World Bank 2006, 61).

Looking at the state of education in the Pacific, one can only conclude that the glass is more empty than full. While there has been some progress in access, there are marked deficiencies in quality, equity, efficiency, and sustainability. And there is a culture of not using information to identify and address underlying causes. Evidence points to the fact that after some progress in the 1990s, there is stagnation and even regression in many areas.

Hypotheses About Underlying Causes

There is a considerable range of hypotheses that have been put forward regarding the reasons for stagnation and decline in the state of education in the Pacific. I discuss ten hypotheses below, but these are by no means exhaustive nor are they mutually exclusive.

Inadequate Funding

One line of argument, now increasingly out of vogue, is that educational outcomes are poor because funding is inadequate. In most PICs, expenditure on education is high due to a combination of large budget allocations and supplementary donor assistance. A 2004 ADB study noted that "whether measured as a proportion of the government's recurrent budget or as a proportion of GDP, many [PICs] have relatively high levels of spending on education…. Frequently, however, increased spending has not fully translated into more or better educational services" (Abbott and Pollard 2004, 33).

For the 11 PICL countries for which budget data were available (circa 2000), education received, on average, 19 percent of the budget (Abbott and Pollard 2004, Table 11). Spending on social services, in general, is higher than in most comparable countries. In 2006, the World Bank reported that "Pacific countries are better resourced than others—on average, governments and donors spend around US$318.80 per capita on [health and education] nearly double that spent in other similar small states" (World Bank, 2006, vii).

> The problem is clearly not inadequate funding; rather, it is that outcomes are not commensurate with expenditure.

The problem is clearly not inadequate funding; rather, it is that outcomes are not commensurate with expenditure. There is increasing concern that money is simply not being spent effectively. "Judging from the resources flowing into education and health," reported the World Bank, "governments have made special efforts. Are the results commensurate?" (World Bank 2006, 22)

Do Pacific Islanders value education?

Others argue that outcomes are poor in some areas of the Pacific islands region because education is not highly valued culturally. At the 22nd Annual Pacific Educational Conference, then US Deputy Assistant Secretary of the Interior David Cohen said, "I'm afraid that people do not truly value education [in the North Pacific]" (Johnson 2005).

There is a substantial literature on Pacific "subsistence affluence" which argues that education is not essential in agrarian economies.

> People who can derive a reasonable living from cocoa and oil palm farming while having good access to nearby towns and good food, are not as stressed to achieve academically (*Post Courier* 2010).

But there is certainly substantial evidence that many Pacific Islanders value education highly. For example, in a 2007 survey of 2,200 people in one PIC, 97.7 percent of respondents agreed that it is very important for all children to go to school (ASPEW 2007, 6).

This is also reflected in reports of migrants who list wanting better education for their children as a motivation to move. In some countries students will repeat the final year of primary school (sometimes several times) to improve examination results and gain entry to high-quality secondary schools (World Bank 2006, 55).

It is also possible that some parents do not value education because they realize that the quality of education is so poor that it will not yield tangible returns. This may simply be a case of not valuing lousy education.

It is clear that elites in PICs value education for their own children and relatives. Abuse of scholarship systems is a common problem in some PICs. A substantial share of expenditure goes for tertiary education and much of that is spent abroad. As one editorial asked, "Why must public funds be spent on educating children of leaders abroad" (*National* 2010)? In another PIC, the press reported that national scholarship funds had been used for the overseas education of the minister of education's daughter and children of several parliamentarians. The allocation process bypassed the normal selection mechanisms and students were sent to study in expensive overseas institutions that were explicitly excluded from consideration because of high costs (Eremae 2005).

> **Abuse of scholarship systems is a common problem in some Pacific Island countries.**

I worked in one country where the unit responsible for scholarship was regularly reprimanded for exceeding the annual budget allocation. However, each year unit staff received instructions from high-ranking parliamentarians to add additional awards for specific students who had not been selected in the normal process. These instructions were endorsed by their own minister.

Mismatch with Pacific culture

A variant on the theme of not valuing education is the argument that the inherited colonial education system is not congruent with Pacific values. That is, "the high failure rate of Pacific islanders to a mode of education which does not relate to their culture and way of life" (*Pacific Daily News* 2011).

While there clearly are issues related to the transplant of education systems from the West, this is not an issue exclusive to education in PICs. In fact, the countries that consistently have the highest performance on international assessments are generally not Western countries.

There have been various attempts to refocus systems to reflect the "Pacific way," such as the 2001 Rethinking Pacific Education Initiative and the associated Pacific Education Research Fund (Sanga 2003). A decade later, the underlying problems remain unresolved.

An alternative version of the congruence argument is that Pacific Island children have difficulty learning linear Western concepts—that they cannot handle the curriculum. This argument is belied by the fact that there are some excellent schools in the region with high standards, even in systems where national standards are extremely low. These examples of excellent outcomes are not limited to private and church schools; there are examples of government schools that also provide excellent outcomes.

This last point is extremely important because it demonstrates that it is possible to have good-quality education in "ordinary" public schools. Hezel called these schools "islands of excellence in a sea of mediocrity" (2001). Clearly, Pacific Island children can learn; it is neither an inherent deficiency in Pacific Island children nor an alien curriculum that is the problem.

> **Some government schools provide excellent outcomes, demonstrating that it is possible to have good-quality education in 'ordinary' public schools.**

The cultural mismatch may have less to do with content and curriculum than with the culture of using the education budget to create "jobs for the boys."

Lack of technical capacity

This hypothesis assumes that some PIC governments lack the capacity to get things done—that education is poor because governments simply cannot get anything done. That simply does not appear to be the case except in instances of social disruption or fragile states. PICs seem quite adept at responding to emergencies—when there is the political will. Examples include responding to frequent natural disasters, reforming public utilities, and upgrading finance systems. If problems have high visibility and urgency, governments do seem to have the capacity to respond. The problem with education deterioration may simply be that it occurs slowly over time and is therefore seen as less urgent.

Over the past two decades, donors have been very keen on investing in capacity building in education. Recently, there is the growing awareness that lack of technical capacity is not the binding constraint. According to a 2007 AusAID education policy paper, "Weak education performance is generally due to underlying problems with resources, structures and incentives rather than simply a lack of technical capacity" (AusAID 2007, 1).

Moreover, capacity at the central ministry or district education office may not be critical to success, since learning occurs at the school. National plans, ministerial conferences, and regional donor initiatives aimed at capacity building probably have little or no influence on those schools able to become "islands of excellence."

Education as a source of public employment

A key question focuses on the real objectives of education systems: Do schools exist to provide quality education to students or are they primarily a means of providing jobs for the boys? Student/teacher ratios in PICs are extremely high relative to international norms (World Bank 2006). It is hypothesized that high levels of aid and limited private-sector opportunities contribute to this pattern (Feeny and Rogers 2008).

One indicator of the relative importance of learning outcomes versus employment creation is the way resources are allocated. The benchmarks of best practice within the Education for All–Fast Track Initiative recommend allocating about 35 percent of the recurrent budget to non-salary inputs. In many PICs, expenditure clearly reflects a bias away from learning inputs to jobs:

> Currently, over 90 percent of primary recurrent education expenditures goes towards teacher salaries; expenditures on quality related inputs and operating costs are by contrast almost non-existent (World Bank 2006, 7).

Not only are staffing levels high, salaries are also high compared to international norms. Comparing a primary teacher's salary to the average per capita gross domestic product (GDP) in Vanuatu shows that a nonqualified, part-time teacher earns over 3.0 times per capita GDP, while a primary-school teacher earns between 4.0 and 6.0 times per capita GDP. Other Pacific countries follow the same trend: in the Republic of the Marshall Islands, primary-school teachers earn salaries around 4.9 times per capita GDP; in Pohnpei, around 4.7 times per capita GDP; and in Fiji, teacher salaries are 4.2 times per capita GDP. These figures are higher than those seen in many developing countries where salaries for qualified primary teachers are around 2.0 times per capita GDP (World Bank 2006, 60).

Also, there are instances where publicly employed teachers are paid more than the official salary scale dictates. One study found that the majority of teachers were being paid more than the legal pay-scale wage; some teachers received more than twice the legal maximum salary (ADB 2010).

Despite high salaries, in some systems there are high levels of teacher absenteeism and limited accountability. Weak information makes it difficult to quantify the extent of the problem. The World Bank has conducted several studies of staff absenteeism in other regions. A recent study of five countries found an average daily absenteeism rate of 19 percent. Absence rates were even higher for employees with greater authority, such as headmasters (Chaudhury et al. 2006). This is consistent with a limited number of ad hoc studies and with general public perceptions about teacher

> **Despite high salaries, in some systems there are high levels of teacher absenteeism and limited accountability.**

attendance in PICs. The issue of teacher absenteeism appears frequently in the popular press (Johnson 2011). One editorial observed that "teachers should not abscond from their postings and wander around the towns and cities picking up their salaries for nothing" (*Post-Courier* 2010a).

During school visits in one PIC, when I observed that there were fewer classes in session than the official registration, I was told that teacher absenteeism is so entrenched that students are instructed not to come to school on days when their teacher plans to be absent. This practice was widespread and acknowledged to be an open secret. Given that teachers regularly do not come to work, it is not surprising that there are high levels of student absenteeism. In one country, it was reported that school maintenance workers were sometimes asked to cover classes for absent teachers (Limtiaco 2003).

Aside from the issue of attendance, there are concerns about teachers' competence. In some countries where there have been staff assessments, results are shocking. For example, in one country, an assessment of the national teaching force, using the high school English exam, found that over 80 percent of the teachers failed either the reading or writing sections of the exam; almost two-thirds (63 percent) failed both parts (Johnson 2004).

There are concerns about teachers' competence. In some countries, staff-assessment results are shocking.

Problems in teacher competence may simply be due to perverse selection criteria. Some argue that in many countries there are qualified and motivated young people who would be happy to accept teaching appointments; they are excluded because they don't have the right connections. It appears that poor quality is not due to the lack of competent candidates; rather, it is caused by fundamental flaws in the selection process.

This is consistent with limited data on private schools, where staffing decisions are typically not in the hands of politicians. While offering lower pay, these schools are able to recruit and retain more competent teachers. A study in one country found that three-quarters of the staff employed in the education sector could not pass the standard high school English examination; however, all staff at two high-performing private schools passed the same examination. What is noteworthy is that salaries at the private schools were only 59 percent of the average paid in the government sector (ADB 2010). The fact that schools paying substantially lower salaries were able to attract more competent teachers strongly suggests that the core problem lies in the public personnel system. Also, international evidence indicates that rates of teacher absenteeism are generally lower at private schools (Chaudhury et al. 2006).

There is substantial literature suggesting that a system of patronage dominates the political economy of the Pacific. The allocation of education funds to individuals constitutes a "targeted transfer" which carries with it the obligation of reciprocity. Provision of quality education is a public good, which cannot be directly related to a specific benefactor (ADB 2010).

The patronage mentality adversely affects education in two ways. First, incompetent and ineffective teachers are hired and retained. Second, the excessive allocation to salaries (90 percent of the recurrent budget) deprives schools of other critical learning-related inputs and funding for maintenance. This misallocation of resources requires school fees to meet these other costs, leading to the exclusion of children from low-income households. Donors have responded to the access issue by funding school grant programs to offset the need for fee income. While this is a socially valuable intervention, it does not address the core problem of excessive allocation of public resources to salaries and, in fact, eliminates incentives for reform. The reliance on donor funding for school grants further increases donor dependency and contributes to financially unsustainable commitments. Donor funding of school grants, while beneficial in the short term, is probably detrimental in the long term. It provides a safety valve to avoid addressing the patronage problem. Testimony to the Australian Senate emphasizes this point in a brief sentence: "Aid flows enabled excessive public employment to be expanded" (Hughes 2002, 3).

> **Reliance on donor funding for school grants further increases donor dependency and contributes to financially unsustainable commitments.**

Weak governance

Of course, problems of patronage are a manifestation of a broader problem of poor governance, which is increasingly recognized as a key constraint to service delivery:

> The quality of services is undermined by a number of issues related to governance. These indicate the need for effective decentralization, achieving greater policy coherence, reducing corruption, strengthening regulations, generating better data, increasing accountability and stakeholder participation (ADB 2010, 2).

The agenda for service expansion has shrunk dramatically in the Pacific, and further investments will prove less effective than new efforts in management and governance (World Bank 2006, 7).

> Governance is critical…. At the community level we will support measures that increase family involvement in school management and raise demand for greater transparency and accountability in service provision (AusAID 2007, 2).

Donors have made substantial investments in improving governance. For Australia, it is estimated that governance-reform projects accounted for more than 30 percent of total overseas development assistance. This figure understates the emphasis on governance within the AusAID budget, as AusAID also spends an estimated 30 percent of the value of its aid to education and 50 percent of its aid to the health sector on significant governance components (Duncan 2010, 140).

Yet, there is increased recognition that donor efforts at improving governance have been largely unsuccessful. A recent ADB study reports that "current governance reform efforts in the Pacific by international aid agencies are not working" (Duncan 2010, 140). The same report tries to identify "why governance reform in the PICs over the past decade or so has been so unsuccessful" and suggests "that 'big man' political culture is currently the main obstacle to governance reforms in the Pacific" (Duncan 2010, 19).

There is an extensive literature on patronage and reciprocity in the Pacific and it is beyond the scope of this paper to fully review the topic. However, it is argued that in some places the culture of the village-level "big man" has evolved into national politics. Some argue that many Pacific societies "are enmeshed in networks of obligation and reciprocity. Therefore, the cultural expectations of their kinsmen compel politicians, government officials, and village big men to access and distribute resources" (Duncan 2010, 26).

> In distributing public resources, the big man acquires the same status and influence as when distributing village resources. The context has changed, but the values have not. Diversion of public resources is often labeled "corruption," but many of these activities are expected of big men. As long as the local big man is diverting public resources to his supporters, and not hoarding them for himself, it is appropriate behavior under traditional cultural norms… . Voters expect big men to divert public resources for their benefit (Duncan 2010, 20).

This is reflected in competition between different players to control the staffing function. There have been numerous newspaper articles describing conflicts between departments of education, public service commissions, boards of education, individual parliamentarians, executive branches, and other power brokers regarding who is empowered to select and/or "protect" teachers. Issues include delays in hiring (Johnson 2011), politically motivated firing (*Pacific Daily News* 2006), and conflicts in responsibility (Johnson 2011).

Governance problems lead directly to waste and inefficiency. One PIC department of education recently underwent a major independent management audit that identified areas for substantial cost savings. The local press reported that "the vast majority of the management audit's recommendations have been ignored, while the…. Department of Education asks for more and more funding." The article goes on to note that the "'there's no money excuse' must not be accepted, especially when there is a blueprint that details exactly what steps the local education agency can take to cut costs and thus free up money for other expenses" (*Pacific Daily News* 2011a).

Various reports have acknowledged that corruption is widespread and that it has a direct and detrimental impact on the quality of education:

> Corruption is believed to be quite widespread in the Pacific (Duncan 2010, 26).

> Corruption in the education sector reduces the resources available for schooling, limiting access and driving down quality, as well as reducing public confidence and demand (AusAID 2007, 14).

No incentives to improve efficiency

Another explanation is that there are no incentives for improvement and, in fact, there are strong disincentives. Policymakers and leaders, who have the power to improve the system, do not suffer the impact of low-quality service:

> Leaders would always have a lackadaisical and cavalier attitude towards provision of decent and quality education or medical services so long as they know they or their kindred can seek both of those services abroad in places like Australia, Singapore and the Philippines (*National* 2010).

School principals have no incentive to identify chronically absent or low-performing teachers as this would be socially disruptive, and school managers are not held accountable for learning outcomes.

School principals have no incentive to identify chronically absent or low-performing teachers.

Moreover, international evidence indicates that in systems with high teacher absenteeism, principals are even more likely to be absent than teachers (Chaudhury et al. 2006).

Teachers also have few incentives to improve efficiency; there are no consequences for poor student outcomes or even for high levels of absenteeism. International studies suggest that teachers are almost never fired for repeated absenteeism. As one analyst observed,

> Given the rarity of disciplinary action for repeated absence, the mystery for economists may not be why absence from work is so high, but why anyone shows up at all (Chaudhury et al. 2006, 93).

Improved accountability would undermine opportunities for patronage.

> It is simply not in the interest of Pacific big men for proper oversight to exist in the ministries that control distribution, as that would hinder their task of distributing resources to their supporters (Duncan 2010, 20).

> Unscrupulous government officials…have stronger personal and political interest in maintaining rather than reforming governance practices (ADB 2010, 1).

Donor support also mitigates against reform.

> Instead of fostering reform, aid incentives may ease domestic pressure for reform by shoring up failing public services, making development of local capacity less necessary, or by providing discretionary goods and services that can be dispensed by unscrupulous politicians as patronage (ADB 2010, 1).

Also, as discussed below, due to competition between donors there are few incentives to press for meaningful reform and accountability.

> The problem is not that development banks are alien to Pacific culture; rather, 'development banks look exactly like a very Pacific concept— the chief's storehouse or the pile of gifts at a feast' (Duncan 2010, 21).

Weak civil society

Another hypothesis is that education is poor because parents and civil society do not exert pressure on governments for decent service delivery. There are several possible explanations as to why PIC civil society appears to be so ineffective.

First, it may be that civil society is unaware of the poor quality of education relative to other countries; they simply don't have the information. There have been a number of attempts by international organizations to strengthen the media and information dissemination. For example, in 2010 the United Nations Educational, Scientific and Cultural Organization (UNESCO) organized a regional workshop to improve media coverage of education issues in the region (Matangi 2010).

Alternatively, there may be a reluctance to criticize leaders or to intrude into the domain of education "experts." In most instances, Pacific Islanders tend to be nonconfrontational and particularly reluctant to challenge authority figures. There is little evidence of the public outrage that would be expressed in other societies. As one official asked, "Could the outrage of parents result in positive change and more money for the schools?... Outrage isn't something we do well in the Pacific" (Johnson 2005). There may be little outrage, as respect for authority is a societal norm.

> **Pacific Islanders tend to be nonconfrontational and particularly reluctant to challenge authority figures.**

> Authoritarian values and traditions sometimes reinforce hierarchical social systems where citizens avoid openly questioning their leaders, and political expectations that view elected politicians as victors with a right to power and the spoils of victory (ADB 2010, 2).

Another reason why there may be limited public outrage at wasteful expenditure, is that the funds are seen as coming from abroad—a kind of "free good."

> Aid funds...reduce pressure on governments to use revenues wisely and to perform well because the revenues are not raised from taxes (Duncan, 2010, 27).

It may also be that civil-society organizations realize that they lack power and that it is not worth challenging entrenched authority. ADB reports on an interesting initiative to strengthen civil society for education reform in one PIC. Substantial information on public sector inefficiency was widely disseminated and "parents called on the government to fire immediately [those staff] not performing up to standards" (ADB 2010, 22). The ultimate outcome was that these recommendations were simply ignored by senior government officials and no meaningful reform ensued.

History of "Grand Remedies"

Problems in Pacific education are not a new story; there is a long history of attempts to redress these problems. It is useful to review some of the major interventions and to assess what has and has not worked. Here, we briefly review six major approaches; the list is not exhaustive, but it does provide a sense of how problems have been approached.

Large infusions of donor funding

On a per capita basis, PICs have received and continue to receive an extremely high level of donor support; education has been one of the priority areas for funding. There is a growing consensus that much of this money has been wasted. Although many individual projects have had a beneficial impact, the overall conclusion is that large infusions of funding have not resulted in significant improvements. There is increasing recognition that in and of itself, more money is not the solution.

> Education has been a priority area for donor funding, yet there is a growing consensus that much of this money has been wasted.

Technical assistance, analysis, and reports

I have authored scores of technical documents, including national plans, evaluation reports, public expenditure reviews, and the like. These are my general impressions regarding the impact of the technical documents I have produced:

- Almost no one in the ministries of education or elsewhere in the governments ever read the documents closely. In some cases, staff members haven't been able to find a copy of the reports a few years later. Sometimes, no one remembers that a study was ever done. Aside from the "easy" recommendations or those imposed by donor agencies, the analyses I have been involved in have had little practical impact on actual practice.
- The funding agencies that paid for the reports read them closely, but only *once*.
- The main audience for the reports is the next wave of external technical experts, who will produce more documents that feed the cycle.

This concern does not go unnoticed in the popular press in donor countries. A recent review of donor assistance reported in the Australian press found that "tens of millions of dollars were being gobbled up and 'wasted' on consultants and glossy reports. Money is also being used to prop up bloated bureaucracies" (*Northern Territory News* 2011).

My general conclusion would be that there are far too many reports and too many international experts arriving on "fly-in" missions. If anything, they are a distraction and a burden on civil servants' time. They generate complex and confusing solutions to what, I will argue later, are fairly basic and easily remedied problems. I am not saying that technical analysis must be useless; it is simply that if it is funded and driven by external agencies, it really has little impact. In my experience, much of the technical assistance has been supply driven. Aid beneficiaries recognize that donors "need" these studies as part of project preparation, and they put up with them in order to receive funding. Long-term, ministry-based technical advisors have been more effective. However, in many cases they are also there to meet the needs of the external donor agencies. There is often little technology transfer or capacity building due to a combination of deadlines on producing deliverables and little genuine domestic demand for these analyses.

National education plans

A sizeable share of donor spending has focused on preparing national education plans. In many PICs there now exists a baffling array of five-year plans, ten-year plans, Vision 2020 documents, corporate plans, action plans, strategic plans, rolling plans, and frameworks. Most of these are funded by external donors and written by expatriate advisers. They are generally unnecessarily long and complex, and they are often peppered with banal vision statements and client charters. Some countries have more than one plan (e.g., a national plan and an Education for All plan); these are duplicative and poorly aligned. A review of Education for All (EFA) plans in 14 PICs found that in 13 countries, the freestanding EFA plan, prepared as a separate document, was not aligned with the national education plan (Young 2011).

> **There now exists a baffling array of five-year plans, ten-year plans, 'Vision 2020' documents, corporate plans, action plans, and more.**

Of course, if there is a real intention to do something, a plan is very helpful. Most of these plans are never fully implemented and many of the indicators and benchmarks call for preparation of yet additional plans and documents. Plans often include targets for enrollment but rarely have quantified quality targets. They focus on inputs but neglect outcomes.

The key point is that, if the plan is not actually going to be implemented, it makes little difference whether it is thick or eloquent. I do not think that this cynicism regarding grand plans escapes the public. An example was the coverage of the Rethinking Conference in one PIC, during which a new draft strategic plan for education was discussed. The local press reported:

> The Rethinking Conference discussed a new draft strategic plan for the Ministry of Education 2007–2011, and injected suggestions into it. But it strains credulity to believe that this can be more successfully implemented than any of the multitude of previous plans in the absence of some major new developments, such as staffing at the ministry, a demand for change by the public, reform of the hiring and firing system (Johnson 2004).

The essence of the problem was captured in a headline describing a 2002 regional education workshop in Suva: "Old Wine in New Bottle." The keynote speaker observed that "Concerns about the management of education raised at this meeting were the same as in the 1970–80 period" (Naidu and Prasad 2002).

In their worst manifestations, elaborate plans actually get in the way of planning. The plan documents are so exhaustive that it becomes difficult to differentiate the important from the trivial. I worked in one Pacific state that had three different education plans prepared over the course of six years. There were so many plans and so many priorities that the country's Department of Education failed to implement key activities that had huge financial implications (Levine 2009).

> **Elaborate plans actually get in the way of planning.**

Regional donor projects

In addition to the direct bilateral and multilateral aid going directly to individual countries, donors have also been enthusiastic about supporting regional education projects. I differentiate here between specific, time-bound projects and the aid that is channeled to various regional organizations. My focus is on two major multi-year donor projects: Basic Education and Literacy Support (BELS) and Pacific Regional Initiatives for the Delivery of Basic Education (PRIDE). BELS ran from 1993 to 2000 and was funded by the United Nations Development Programme, UNESCO, United Nations Children's Fund, AusAID, and New Zealand Official Development Assistance. PRIDE ran from 2004 to 2009, funded by the European Union and AusAID.

Given the time that has elapsed since BELS, there is a surprisingly limited amount of documentation available. It is interesting that a fairly broad search of library databases, as well as searches of the websites of the agencies that funded BELS, turned up only scant reference to the ten-year, five-agency project. It is not clear why this regional initiative left so light a mark on development literature. For some reason (speculation on my part), it appears that the development community may not be keen to recall BELS. Clearly, one major contribution of BELS was that it provided quantitative evidence of the extent of the deficiencies in education in the region. PRIDE was more recent and better documented. Funding for a second phase of PRIDE was not approved and the project ended in 2009.

Like competing donor organizations, regional projects have had to find an audience for their services. In some cases, it has appeared to be supply searching for demand. PRIDE, whose central mandate was to assist in developing national plans, had an added component for providing "open grants" of US$100,000 per country, which perhaps reflected the dual objectives of "being responsive to local priorities" and "buying access." More than half of total PRIDE funding ended up being allocated to approximately 140 separate national sub-projects. It is somewhat ironic that what was to have been an integrative regional approach, ended up funding an array of disjointed projects and sub-projects—an approach that is generally seen as ineffective by the international community. Among some development professionals, PRIDE was derisively referred to as "the ATM project."

> **Regional projects have had to 'find an audience' for their services. In some cases, it appeared to be supply searching for demand.'**

While it would be unfair to dismiss regional projects as ineffective (they have had some positive impacts), it would be a mistake to think that these education initiatives have had a major impact in addressing the fundamental problems. At best, the impacts have been marginal and inadequate. If these regional projects had made a significant difference, there would be evidence or progress rather than regression in the region. The fact that PRIDE funding was not extended for a proposed second phase is an indication that funding agencies recognized its limited impact and effectiveness.

While there are some issues that are probably best addressed through a regional perspective, large multi-country projects face the danger of being reduced to the lowest common denominator. It is difficult to get consensus on reforms or standards that actually have teeth. And, aside from gaining access, there is little benefit in spreading money around.

Regional meetings and ministerial initiatives

There are numerous regional forums where education is discussed. These typically generate high-level statements endorsing broad principles, followed by little substantive action—a great deal of talk and few results.

The problem was well-summarized by the New Zealand minister of foreign affairs at an event in September 2011. Minister Murray McCully said, "We need to get out of 'business as usual' mode and get serious about tackling the issues that have attracted a good deal of talk at regional meetings in the past but too little action and follow-through afterwards" (Young 2011a).

The highest-visibility meeting on education is the Forum of Education Ministers Meetings (FEdMM), which has been held periodically since 2001; to date, there have been a total of seven meetings. At the initial meeting the ministers adopted the Forum Basic Education Action Plan (FBEAP), which has been amended at subsequent meetings. In 2008, the ministers requested that the Pacific Islands Forum Secretariat (PIFS) undertake a comprehensive review of the FBEAP, including PRIDE activities. Of course, the report (PIFS 2009) put a positive spin on the FEdMM/FBEAP process; however, details provided in the report paint a fairly bleak picture. Combined with various amendments, the FBEAP grew to a 40-page document; the original plan identified 15 priority areas and plans of action. Subsequent meetings added an additional six priorities. In my experience, when everything is a priority there are no priorities.

> **When everything is a priority there are no priorities.**

The PIFS study found that the FBEAP document was "unwieldy and not user-friendly," that many senior government officials had "not read it or were unaware as to how to obtain a copy," and that the "FBEAP has not been prominent at all in policy and planning dialogue at the national level." The review also found that the "FBEAP was much more widely known amongst regional agencies and other development partners" (PIFS 2009, 25). This, of course, raises concerns about the real purpose for, and constituency of, these regional meetings.

One of the main recommendations of the review was that the "action plan" be rewritten and presented as a "framework." One cannot help but be reminded of the headline "Old Wine in New Bottle."

Capacity building

Initiatives in capacity building are, of course, premised on the assumption that the intention to implement reforms exists and that inadequate capacity is the constraint. In the education sector, these capacity-building initiatives have generally focused on training for central ministry staff, new information systems (discussed separately below), and investments in teacher training. PRIDE had been the major mechanism for capacity building under the FBEAP and eight of the PICL countries have explicit capacity-building components in their national education plans (PIFS 2009, 23).

In many cases, capacity building takes the form of technical assistance. It is estimated that about half of AusAID program spending is for technical assistance; that is about twice the average spent by the Organisation for Economic Co-operation and Development (OECD) for technical assistance (Lowy Institute 2008). Observers note that, while beneficiary countries are reluctant to refuse technical assistance, this is probably not really their highest priority. "[M]ost Pacific Island countries [would prefer] to see more donor investment in tangible projects that have a more visible direct impact on the population than capacity-building programs, the benefits of which are difficult to translate for public consumption" (Lowy Institute 2008). High levels of spending on technical assistance also generate resentment in some PICs. "The huge payments to foreign aid consultants have triggered major protests from countries such as PNG, Tonga, Solomon Islands and other recipients of Australian aid" (Lewis 2011a).

Capacity building does, of course, greatly facilitate the work of donor organizations. Improved procurement processes help to absorb funding and document conformity to agency procurement guidelines, data are more readily available, logistics of annual joint reviews are better managed, and reports are better written. In my experience, donors often interact primarily with their long-term resident advisers (now typically called "sector coordinators"), who are based in ministries. The old "projectimplementation unit" model has been discontinued, but nowadays there is often a "project-management unit" which has many of the same characteristics. In most countries, civil servants do not make policy, they implement policies set by politicians. Therefore, strengthening bureaucratic capacity has limited impact if the core problem is perverse incentives and bad policy.

> **Strengthening bureaucratic capacity has limited impact if the core problem is perverse incentives and bad policy.**

Donors are also very keen on teacher training and upgrading teacher credentials. Most annual donor reports include information on the number of teachers trained. This is easy to count and easy to report, but as discussed in a later section on international evidence, there is little reason to believe that these training activities improve student-learning outcomes.

Education management information systems

One of the central elements of capacity-building initiatives has been the creation of education management information systems (EMIS). Typically, an EMIS contains data submitted by schools on enrollment, staffing, facilities, and related information. This is usually maintained in a relational database, such as Access, and systems include historic information that can be used to study trends over time. I do not recall working in any ministry of education over the past ten years or so that did not have an EMIS. However, I have worked in a number of countries, including PICs, where the EMIS is weak or dysfunctional.

Clearly, it makes a great deal of sense to use computers to manage information and conduct analysis. Most staff in ministries of education have decent computer skills and regularly use spreadsheets for data manipulation. So, why are EMIS data underutilized for policy analysis and research, and even for planning and management?

In my experience, the systems are often over-designed. It is not uncommon for a donor to spend a million dollars or more developing a system—typically contracting with an organization in its own country. The systems are so complex that contracts are extended with ongoing support from expatriate advisers. Today, in virtually every country, including very small PICs, there is sufficient private-sector local capacity to design and support a workable system using inexpensive, off-the-shelf software, but this is very seldom the case.

Some of these EMIS systems were designed and are only used to produce one annual statistical report; they are simply not used for management. They automatically generate an array of UNESCO statistics. In many cases, a ministry produces an annual statistical abstract or annexes of tables for its annual report. Hardly anyone actually looks at these statistics or considers what they imply about the efficiency of the system.

> **Hardly anyone actually looks at these statistics or considers what they imply about the efficiency of the system.**

In one PIC, I discovered that, despite the existence of an expensive EMIS, the education system was still managed using a system of written ledgers. Whenever information was required, the planning unit retrieved a bound ledger from the shelf. This was a small school system and the ledgers worked well. The EMIS program was run once a year to generate a report. But, the automatic construction of indicators was actually an impediment to having anyone think about what the data really meant. Donors like to have comparable indicators to include in international databases, and an EMIS can provide them.

An additional issue is that EMIS data are often incomplete, incorrect, or out of date. Schools are required to complete annual (or more frequent) survey forms. Within many PIC education systems, no information flows back to the schools and, over time, the quality of data deteriorates. There are frequently no checks for consistency and no consequences for providing incorrect information or for not submitting the survey returns. Many EMIS systems are designed to use data from an earlier year to populate the file, if no return is received. I worked in one country where the data from the most expensive government school were eight years old. Figures had automatically cascaded forward from 2004, the last time a return had been completed.

In too many instances, capacity building is a solution that is unrelated to the core problem. The existence of an expensive and sophisticated EMIS does not mean that management has improved. In many countries there now exist rich databases, but they are not used for research, planning, policy analysis, or even for management. Thousands of teachers can be channeled through training activities, but unless there is evidence that the training has a positive impact on student learning, it probably reflects a poor use of resources. In the absence of incentives, capacity building appears to have little impact.

Donors

On a per capita basis, aid to PICs is extremely high; arguably the highest in the world. Official development assistance (ODA) has been on the order of about one billion dollars annually in recent years. This estimate excludes donor flows that are not reported in the OECD Development Assistance Committee system; unreported flows from China and Taiwan are substantial (AusAID 2009).

Data on ODA per capita are available for 149 countries; 11 of which are PICL states. The average for these 11 PICL states is US$542 per capita, compared to US$110 for the other 138 recipient countries—a difference of almost five to one (World Bank 2011). Testimony to the Australian Senate committee on foreign affairs in 2002 suggested even higher ratios, on the order of six to one (Hughes 2002).

In many PICs, external assistance represents an extremely large share of the overall economy. For 14 PICL countries receiving ODA, external assistance in 2007 represented 35 percent of GDP, on average (AusAID 2009, Table 11), with Australia as the largest donor. A substantial share of ODA in the Pacific is directed at supporting education. OECD data suggest that, on average, per capita support to education in Oceania was US$265 per annum during the period 2006 to 2009.

Because donors provide an atypically large share of finance to education in PICs, it is useful to consider the role and incentives of donor agencies. The popular perception is that being in the business of "giving money away" would be a low-stress occupation. Nothing could be further from the truth. I have worked either as an employee or a consultant for at about 20 donor organizations, and it is an extremely competitive business. Despite rhetoric to the contrary, success is measured by "moving money," not by outcomes and results. All the rhetoric of Paris Accords harmonization aside, donors continue to be in direct competition, and at times, the competition can be ruthless. In some countries, it is a case of supply chasing demand. A recent review of the Forum Basic Education Action Plan (FBEAP) noted that "some countries are experiencing difficulties in actually absorbing the extra funding from donors" (PIFS 2009, 57).

In the Pacific, due to the easy availability of bilateral grant assistance, multinational organizations such as the World Bank and ADB have had difficulty in marketing loans, even on highly concessional terms. The ADB has instituted policies of increasing grant assistance to the Pacific and has established institutional incentives.

A recent study by the US Congressional Budget Office noted the perception that

> there are disincentives for donor coordination at every level of foreign assistance policy making and implementation.... Aid agencies may fear that increased collaboration will mean less independence and that more efficiency will mean downsizing (Lawson 2010, 15).

There is growing concern that aid to education in the Pacific is simply not effective. There is particular concern about this among regional bilateral donors: "Millions of dollars of New Zealand aid to be used to educate children in the South Pacific is misspent, says an Oxfam report published in a leading New Zealand newspaper" (PINA Nius Online 2001).

A paper recently commissioned by AusAID notes that "aid has not had the impact in the [Pacific] region that it should have had" and that it is "not safe to assume that aid will always have a positive impact" (ASPBAE 2011, 185). Expert testimony to the Australian Senate was even more pessimistic: "Aid is…not the solution to Pacific development, but a major part of the problem" (Hughes 2002).

There is growing pressure on donor organizations to actually demonstrate impacts; this is especially true in the Pacific region where past experience has been disappointing. There is an increasing incidence of "donor fatigue" and, in the short run, this will probably intensify in the context of the 2008 global financial crisis and debt crises in the United States and Eurozone. The popular press does report evidence of this perception:

> Australia's foreign aid program is under siege following revelations that tens of millions of dollars are being wasted on mega-salaries for consultants and rich contracts for private firms (*Northern Territory News* 2011).

> While these children go begging, your tax dollars go to waste (Lewis and Christensen 2010).

Despite evidence of ineffective use of donor funds, until quite recently most agencies were unwilling to take a strong stand on insisting on greater accountability. Among bilateral agencies, there was the feeling that they could depend on the multilateral agencies, such as the World Bank and ADB, to insist on strong "conditionality" to promote reform. This, of course, turned out to be ill-advised. There still appears to be more money on offer than can be absorbed. Multinationals are disadvantaged in several ways. First, in general, they are offering loans (on highly concessional terms) in competition with grants. Second, they are perceived as being more difficult and demanding. Even when grant funding is available under entities such as the World Bank-administered Global Partnership for Education (formerly the Education for All–Fast Track Initiative), the application and appraisal processes are often seen as too arduous. It is difficult to move even this grant funding. The greatest obstacle is that, like staff in bilateral agencies, professionals in the multilateral agencies are also in the business of "moving money." The conundrum was well summarized in testimony to the Australian Senate almost a decade ago:

> **Even when grant funding is available, the application and appraisal processes are often seen as too arduous.**

> We can not rely, as we had hoped, on the World Bank (or the Asian Development Bank) to take the burden of conditionality to make aid effective. Experience of these two Banks' lending has shown that their main concern is with their own growth (Hughes 2002).

In recent years, donor agencies have taken a more active role in attempting to address governance issues, and evidence suggests that they have not been very successful in the Pacific. Australia is the largest donor in the region and it boasts that "education is a flagship of the Australian aid program." (AusAID 2010, 1). A brief review of that nation's latest performance report on the education sector (AusAID 2010) provides interesting insights into the difficulties Australia has encountered in trying to support reforms in education in the Pacific. Table 1 of the report shows progress in meeting program goals by objectives in 2009, the most recent year available. Progress is classified as either *green* ("will be fully achieved") or *amber* ("will be partly achieved"). My interpretation of amber is that it is "problematic."

The table presents assessments on the status of 23 projects (or components/objectives within projects). Fourteen of the projects (61 percent) are in the Pacific region. Overall, 10 projects (44 percent) were rated as amber in 2009. However, there are marked differences between the Pacific region and other geographic areas where AusAID supports education. In the Pacific region, 56 percent of projects are rated as amber, compared to 36 percent elsewhere. Clearly, support to education in the Pacific is more problematic.

It is also interesting to look at the focus of ten amber projects: nine out of ten relate to reforms in "soft" areas, rather than the typical brick-and-mortar projects that were in vogue in the past. Clearly, donor organizations are having great difficulty in engaging with efficiency and reform issues.

Of course, the jobs-for-the-boys mentality is not limited to PIC governments. It would be naïve to think that participation in the donor industry is driven entirely by altruism; development is big business and there are strong, vested interests promoting expansion. In Australia, it is estimated that "the amount paid to the big-three private contractors has doubled to $1.8 billion.... Australian universities are also cashing in" (Lewis 2011).

Concern is also raised about the remuneration of individual consultants:

> Aid experts also have questioned the size of contracts paid to "briefcase" advisers who fly into poor countries (Lewis and Christensen 2010).

> More than a dozen aid consultants are earning more than Prime Minister Kevin Rudd, flying around the Pacific to advise on [various topics] (Lewis and Christensen 2010).

Interestingly, despite public recognition that aid is not the solution and may be part of the problem, donors continue to increase funding to the sector. In September 2011, for example, New Zealand Prime Minister John Key announced a new Australia and New Zealand joint initiative to increase education aid to the Pacific (Xinhua News Agency 2011).

Migration

Urban migration is a major demographic factor impacting the education sector in most PICs. In 14 of the 19 PICL countries for which data are available, growth in urban population exceeds rural growth. This is occurring despite the fact that birthrates are typically higher in rural areas. In four of the five countries where the rural-population growth rate is higher, there are high levels of international migration. Migration from urban areas to international destinations is lowering the urban growth rate in these countries.

While it might be argued that there is little need for education for subsistence farmers in outer islands, urban dwellers certainly do need basic literacy and numeracy skills. Patterns of internal migration suggest a growing need for a viable education system. Although, in the absence of economic growth, there may be few opportunities in the formal sector, except for those who obtain public-service employment.

Even if one assumes that there are limited or even zero returns to education in the local economy, quality education has important potential returns for those who migrate. In a number of PICs, there are high levels of emigration. In general, the education system does not provide skills required by emigrants to prosper in destination countries or for their children to succeed in school. A recent ADB study noted that one of the priorities should be to "equip people to go abroad by improving the education system and training" (Duncan 2010, 136).

I raised this issue during consulting missions in two PICs that have high levels of emigration. In both cases, senior education officials preferred not to acknowledge that the education system had a responsibility to those who might emigrate. In one country, I was taken aside and informed that the subject was taboo.

Many Pacific Islanders who emigrate do not return; they need an educational foundation that will prepare them for life and employment in the global economy.

> A distinctive feature of international migration in the Pacific is that migrants have typically tended to be settlers, rather than temporary migrants, even though they may express (and sometimes act on) intentions to return home (Brown and Jimenez 2008, 548).

For those PICs with significant emigration, remittances have an enormous economic impact. A recent study based on household survey data suggests that in Tonga 90 percent of households receive remittance income; in Fiji, the estimate is 60 percent (Brown and Jimenez 2008, 549). Clearly, the quality of education at home has an enormous impact on employment and earnings outcomes following migration and, by extension, on remittances and national income.

> For those Pacific Island countries with significant emigration, remittances have an enormous economic impact.

It is not clear how remittances affect income distribution. Early in the process, as substantial migration begins, it appears that better-educated individuals from higher-income households are more likely to emigrate with remittances, thus increasing income inequality. Over time, participation broadens and more lower-income households send migrants and receive remittances, improving the income distribution. Overall, at all stages, remittances lower poverty levels (Brown and Jimenez 2008). There is some evidence that the poor quality of social services at home is one of the factors motivating emigration (Hart 2009).

Children of immigrants from PICs generally experience difficulty in school. In part, this may due to language problems, but much has to do with the poor quality of education at home. This imposes substantial additional costs on the host countries, including some PICL states. In 2009, it was estimated that "Hawaii has spent more than $100 million every year on services to the 12,000 [Compact of Free Association] migrants" (Hart 2009). By 2011, the estimated number of compact migrants increased to 20,720, an increase of over 70 percent, and the cost of education services alone for these individuals was estimated at US$55 million (Hart 2011).

Policies and funding of social services have implications for migration patterns between PICs:

> Hawai'i's state legislature recently decided to slash funding for healthcare services to citizens of the Marshall Islands, Palau, and the Federated States of Micronesia who have migrated to that state because of the Compact of Free Association agreement.... The chief concern centers on the possibility of increased migration of Micronesian residents from Hawai'i to Guam if such a cut were to happen (Hart 2009).

International Evidence on What Works

In the first issue of Pacific Islands Policy, Hezel discusses the shifts in evidence and theory regarding economic growth and changes in underlying assumptions about causal links. A parallel process has occurred in education; there have been significant shifts in education evidence, theory, and assumptions about what works, particularly over the past ten years. Unfortunately, policy, practice, and even the expert advice from many donor agencies have not kept pace with findings of empirical research. I stress that it would be a mistake to look for a new magic bullet to improve education in PICs. The impact of policies and strategies is constrained by the overarching limitations of intention and political will. However, many current practices in PICs are inconsistent with emerging empirical evidence, and this provides a point of reference for considering change.

> **It would be a mistake to look for a new magic bullet to improve education in Pacific Island countries.**

As discussed earlier, data and research on education in PICs are limited. The most complete and reliable data are from OECD countries, and substantial research has also been conducted in developing countries in other regions. It is not clear that research from other regions can, or should, influence policy in PICs. However, in the absence of PIC-specific research, it is useful to review insights from work in other regions and consider how they might apply to PICs.

Spending

Already mentioned is the fact that on a per capita basis spending on education is extremely high in most PICs, consuming almost 20 percent of recurrent budgets and heavily subsidized by external donor support. The underlying assumption is that higher spending will lead to better outcomes. This was often reflected in donor conditionality regarding education's share of national budgets and insistence that donor funds are additive.

International research shows that there is little consistent evidence (in developing, medium-income, or even high-income countries) that levels of spending are related to student performance, as measured by international assessments or time-series analysis within countries. Higher expenditure certainly does not guarantee better results.

> Efforts to improve education in both the developed and developing world typically focus on providing more inputs to schools—increasing spending along existing allocation patterns. But, substantial evidence

shows that increased funding is not sufficient for improved learning outcomes. Incremental funds may be allocated to inputs that have weak impacts on student learning (World Bank 2011a, 2).

Researchers have documented the weak correlation between spending and results in education that emerge from cross-country and within-country analysis—whether measured in terms of aggregate spending as a share of GDP, spending per student, or trends over time (Bruns, Filmer, and Patrinos 2011, 5).

Teacher credentials

There have been substantial investments in teacher training in PICs and efforts to assure that all or most teachers are certified. In some instances, disbursement of donor assistance is contingent on developing and implementing plans for universal teacher certification. The underlying assumption is that trained teachers (teachers with credentials), are more effective.

A substantial body of correlational studies generally finds little evidence of a relationship between credentials or training and teacher effectiveness. In a study of international assessment results in 21 countries, authors provided the following observation, which is representative of many correlational studies:

> The most striking result is the weak or even absent correlation of achievement test scores and teacher education and professional training (Fehrler, Michaelowa, and Wechtler 2009).

There have been a number of "natural experiments" where certified and uncertified teachers taught in similar circumstances. The general finding is that completion of a formal preservice program has little or no effect on student outcomes. Kane, Rockoff, and Staiger (2008), for example, tracked 50,000 new teachers in New York City. Forty six percent of the teachers were certified, 34 percent were not, and the rest were recruited through alternative schemes with very limited training. Training and certification did not have a significant effect.

A major four-year study in the United States found that teacher-training programs were generally ineffective (Levine 2006). It is a high-income industry involving over 1,400 institutions; one-quarter of all master's degrees in the United States are in education. The report has provided the basis for a new federal-government initiative to completely reform teacher training:

> [The] Obama administration is calling for an overhaul of college programs that prepare teachers, saying they are cash cows that do a mediocre job of preparing teachers for the classroom (Associated Press 2009).

In 2009, US Secretary of Education Arne Duncan called for revolutionary change, saying, "We should be…encouraging the lowest performers to shape up or shut down (Associated Press 2009).

Staffing and class size

On average, PICs allocate a disproportionate share of the recurrent budget to teachers' salaries. The implicit assumption is that more teachers, which result in smaller classes and lower teacher-student ratios, yield better student results.

Research findings are mixed; there is no consistent pattern indicating that (within a reasonable range) learning outcomes are better in smaller classes. There are many individual country studies that do show positive results associated with smaller class size. Other studies show mixed results within countries, differing by province (Corak and Lauzon 2009). A large number of country studies show no effect (Leuven, Oosterbeek, and Ronning 2008). There are also some country-specific studies that indicate a negative effect of smaller classes (Urquiola 2006; Asadullah 2005). However, multicountry studies and meta-analyses tend to consistently indicate that class size does not matter (Woessmann 2005). The research on class size has been characterized as sending mixed messages (Rockoff 2009; Borland, Howsen, and Trawick 2005). In those studies where a statistically significant relationship is found, the impact is generally quite small and, even if positive, unpersuasive on cost-effectiveness grounds (Funkhouser 2009). Increasingly, research suggests that it is more effective to have larger classes with better teachers than to reduce class size (Rivkin, Hanushek, and Kain 2005). Also, the high performance of East Asian students on international assessments, where class sizes have traditionally been high, is often cited as additional evidence (Tang and Williams 2000).

Multi-country studies and meta-analyses tend to consistently indicate that class size does not matter.

Findings on spending, credentials, and class size can be summarized as follows:

It appears that there is only very limited evidence for the effectiveness of intensively debated and costly measures such as reducing class size, increasing academic-qualification requirements, and increasing teachers' salaries (Michaelowa and Wittmann 2007).

Flexible labor markets

In many PICs, there simply is not a labor market for teachers; teachers are centrally selected, often on the basis of patronage, and once employed cannot be fired. The implicit (or perhaps, explicit) assumptions are that (1) staffing decision should be centrally managed and that individual schools and communities should have little or no say, and (2) individuals should not be allowed to compete for teaching positions on the basis of demonstrated performance.

Empirical evidence indicates that there are opportunities for substantial improvements in efficiency and learning gains by identifying ineffective teachers and removing them from the system. Research indicates that transferring students to other classes with effective teachers (even when this increases class size) can have an important positive impact. Moreover, lifetime job tenure removes incentives for teachers to be more productive. A number of studies have found that contract teachers, with lower levels of credentials and lower pay, can actually be more effective than higher-paid, civil-service employees, particularly when staffing decisions are localized to the school.

> In those cases where contract teachers are directly hired and supervised by school-level committees with parent participation—a common formula—the reform also strengthens client power by giving parents and community members a degree of direct authority over teachers that they previously lacked (World Bank 2011a, 19).

Teacher attrition

An important aspect of the labor-market issue is termination and attrition. In PICs (and many countries around the world) teachers are effectively guaranteed lifetime employment. The implicit assumption is that teaching should be an attractive, lifetime occupation. Teacher attrition results in lower quality, and policies should be designed to retain teachers.

There is growing evidence that, for whatever reasons, some people—regardless of training, interest, and good intentions—are simply not effective teachers. Attrition, based on measures of teacher effectiveness, may actually be one of the best strategies for improving student outcomes. Research suggests that rapid assessment, coupled with the termination of new teachers, early in their careers, may be the most cost-effective strategy for increasing student learning (Yen and Ritter 2009; Bressoux, Kramarz, and Prost 2009; McKee, Rivkin, and Sims 2010). In an interesting analysis of US data, it was postulated that eliminating the least effective 5 to 8 percent of teachers and replacing them with average teachers "could move the U.S. near the top of international math and science rankings with a present value [of future student earnings] of US$100 trillion" (Hanushek 2010).

Accountability and incentives

In many PICs, accountability systems are weak or nonexistent and there are few incentives for good performance and no sanctions for failures in service delivery. The implicit assumptions are that (1) the quality of service delivery doesn't matter, (2) incentives don't make a difference, or (3) accountability systems cannot be put in place.

Empirical research increasingly indicates that "improved performance and measurable outcomes depend on a careful balance between three policy instruments that influence the behavior of local actors: (i) greater autonomy at the local level; (ii) enforcing relationships of *accountability;* and (iii) effective *assessment* systems" (World Bank 2011a, 33).

Supply-side financing and government service delivery

While in many PICs there is substantial provision of education by church and private providers, in most the government directly manages public schools. There are few examples of public-private partnerships or charter-school arrangements, where government provides finance but is not directly responsible for management and service delivery. The underlying assumption (common in many countries) is that because education is a public good, government should be responsible for service delivery.

While there is a strong rationale for government financing of basic education, there is increasing evidence that demand-side financing may be more efficient than direct government provision. Moreover, centralized management appears to have a detrimental effect on efficiency. There is an association across countries between good performance on international student achievement tests and local- and school-level autonomy.

> [G]reater autonomy at the provider level, together with competition for resources (e.g., through the use of performance incentives or vouchers), can generate strong provider motivation to improve service delivery (World Bank 2011a, 29).

High subsidies for tertiary students

In most PICs, tertiary education is highly subsidized with generous scholarships financed both through government budgets and directly by donors. The implicit assumption is that subsidies promote equitable access and assure that cost and family income do not constitute a barrier to access

International research shows that in almost all countries, subsidies to higher education are highly regressive. New systems of income-contingent loans are generally seen as a more efficient and equitable approach to addressing access issues. See ADB (2009) for an extensive discussion of issues and options.

Education and economic growth

In many PICs, efforts focus on access but not on quality. Rate-of-return analyses have consistently shown that investments in education (and basic education, in particular) yield high rates of return (Psacharopolous and Patrinos 2002). Initiatives to improve access in many PICs are intended, in part, to alleviate poverty through economic growth. The implicit assumption is that increasing access to schooling and years of schooling completed are effective in reducing poverty through economic growth. However, as noted by Hezel in the first issue of Pacific Islands Policy, there is some question as to whether economic growth is actually a policy objective in some PICs.

A large body of research has consistently found a strong relationship between years of schooling and economic outcomes. However, it is becoming increasingly clear that years of schooling is an imperfect proxy measure of learning and competencies. When actual measures of knowledge (measured by assessment instruments) are included in growth models, the impact of years of schooling is diminished or disappears (Hanushek and Woessmann 2008; World Bank 2011a). The implications for evaluation, planning, and policy analysis are profound. The various international indicators, which measure the flow of bodies through the system, are not adequate. There is a need for reliable measures of learning gains, and this information needs to be collected on a regular basis. If, as is the case for many Pacific Island children, students complete primary or secondary education but are functionally illiterate, it is likely that there will be little or no economic return to the years spent sitting in a dysfunctional school.

> **There is a need for reliable measures of learning gains.**

Countable inputs as proxy quality/outcome indicators

In many PICs, system performance and quality are measured by proxy counts of the inputs flowing into the system (e.g., expenditure, classrooms constructed, teachers trained, and textbooks procured). This is reinforced by donor agencies, who like to report trends in countables in their evaluation reports. There is little direct assessment of actual learning gains or labor-market outcomes. The implicit assumption is that inputs are a reliable proxy for quality and, by extension, outcomes.

A growing body of literature emphasizes the need for directly measuring outcomes and impacts, rather than input proxies, and evaluating alternatives within an equity and cost-effectiveness framework:

> A…willingness by…policy makers to subject new reforms to rigorous evaluations of their impacts and cost effectiveness. Impact evaluation strengthens accountability because it exposes whether programs achieve desired results, who benefits, and at what public cost (Bruns, Filmer, and Patrinos 2011).

Encouraged by donor agencies, there has been overemphasis on a broad array of international education indicators which focus on counting classrooms, "bottoms on benches," and teachers participating in training, rather than student learning. Measuring learning gains is not difficult and need not be costly, and it is becoming increasingly clear that it essential to use "learning gains as a key metric of quality" (World Bank, 2011a).

In summary, in many PICs observed policy and practice seems to reflect assumptions that are at odds with international evidence. There is still an ongoing trend of increasing funding, although it is already extremely high and has not had much impact in the past. Some countries, with encouragement and finance from donors, are assuming that the solution will lie in upgrading credentials. Again, international evidence does not suggest that this will be effective. An excessive share of most budgets goes for staff, and there is, at best, mixed evidence that adding teachers makes a difference.

Outside the private sector, there is no functioning labor market for teachers and very little attrition of nonperforming teachers. Accountability systems are weak or nonexistent due, in part, to the underutilization of assessment data where they are available. In the absence of accountability mechanisms, there are few incentives for performance. There is centralized management and supply-side financing, with few mechanisms for competition for public resources. Tertiary education is heavily subsidized and there are many indications that finance is regressive with advantages captured by elites.

Due to the low quality of learning outcomes, it is unlikely that investments in education are contributing to poverty alleviation.

There is little interest, and some resistance, to collecting data on equity. Due to the low quality of learning outcomes, it is unlikely that investments in education are contributing to poverty alleviation through their contribution to economic growth. Data systems and reports continue to focus on inputs that are easy to count, and they use this information as proxies for progress. Very few systems actually measure "value added" to student outcomes, and this further undermines options for accountability and efficiency improvements. Many donor projects and programs seem to be based on these questionable assumptions, and there is replication of interventions that have failed to work in the past.

Options for Reform

This report has presented substantial commentary on what has not worked with some speculation as to underlying causes. After arguing here against external "experts," it would be ludicrous for me to offer recommendations on reform. Rather, I would like to share a few general thoughts on key issues and suggest options that Pacific Island leaders might want to consider.

The summary presented at the end of the last section paints a fairly bleak picture of prospects for improving education in some PICs. A range of major reform initiatives have provided, at best, mixed results. External donor organizations have not been effective in addressing even the most straightforward issues and the imposition of "conditionality" and sanctions has often been counterproductive. Grand remedies and multicountry regional programs, while doing some good, have failed to address core problems.

I begin this section with my personal, nontechnical assessment of the core problems impeding education in many countries in the region. My observations are somewhat blunt and certainly not "politically correct."

Research findings of the past decade consistently show that the teacher is the single most important school-based determinant of learning outcomes. The core problem in many PICs seems to be poor teacher quality and low productivity; many students are not learning because their teachers are not teaching effectively. Some teachers simply do not have core content competencies; they cannot teach what they do not know, and they should never have been hired in the first place. Others may have limited incentive or motivation; they cannot be fired and are protected either through connections or the inertia of public employment systems that lack accountability.

> **Many students are not learning because their teachers are not teaching effectively.**

Some teachers have the content competency and motivation but, for whatever reasons, are not effective teachers. Most research indicates that when teachers are competent and motivated, with incentives and accountability systems in place, students do learn. Research also indicates that effective teachers do not have to have credentials.

Learning occurs in the classroom. National plans, consultant reports, regional projects, ministerial conferences, and the like (all of which are quite remote from the classroom) are unlikely to have much impact, if teachers are ineffective. The core problem seems to be personnel policies. If teaching positions are allocated and protected on the basis of patronage rather than productivity, there is little prospect for improvement. I believe that the starting point is getting bad teachers out of the system and replacing them with individuals who can *demonstrate* that they are able to teach effectively. Given the high share of expenditure allocated to salaries, there is probably also a need to reduce the total size of the teaching force, with a reallocation of some resources to other learning-related inputs. Either change (replacing teachers or reducing the salary share of the budget) would obviously be socially and politically disruptive. However, as discussed below, the social disruption would only be transitory.

Therefore, the most essential change is moving from a culture where the education system is used to create jobs for the boys to one where the core objective is student learning. Individuals who are able to help children learn are retained as teachers; those who do not perform are replaced. It is essentially a model of payment for performance. This requires a fundamental shift in assessment, moving from counting inputs to actually measuring annual increases in student performance—value added. If employment is contingent on productivity, other problems such as teacher attendance, motivation, principal supervision, and more will take care of themselves; there would be incentives for teacher performance, which are currently lacking in many PICs.

I suggest the criterion of value added rather than specific levels of student competency at the end of each grade. Overall student performance will differ between students for a range of valid reasons that are beyond the control of teachers. Children from economically disadvantaged backgrounds perform less well. At higher grades, end-of-year student performance is strongly influenced by the skills and competencies that students had at the end of the previous year. It would be unrealistic and unfair to expect secondary-school teachers to reach common performance standards at schools where primary-school graduates lack basic skills. It is possible, though, to set reasonable targets for learning gains over each year, controlling for other factors and using this information as a basis for assessing teacher productivity. This approach is being implemented in a number of education systems in other countries.

A transition to performance-based teacher assessment requires reliable measures of student performance. Instruments to obtain this information probably already exist for selected grades in a number of PICs, but the information is generally not used for teacher assessment or policy analysis and is often not made public. It would take time and resources to develop a comprehensive national-assessment system, but, if there is the political will to do so, the process would be manageable.

> **Performance-based teacher assessment requires reliable measures of student performance.**

The key issue, therefore, is whether there are incentives and political will to bring about meaningful change and accountability. The issue of political will could be approached by considering three interrelated questions:

- What are the incentives for change?
- Is it socially and politically feasible to restructure staffing policies and practices?
- If so, how might a national leader manage that process?

Incentives

What are the incentives to change and do they apply in PICs? Many countries in other parts of the world are currently attempting education reform, and it is useful to consider the factors driving reform efforts elsewhere and the extent to which they really apply to PICs. At the moment, two central themes in other countries seem to be *quality* and *efficiency*—both of which have strong economic implications.

The quality issue reflects, in part, concerns about international competitiveness; countries are worried about falling behind competitors due to inadequate human capital. The efficiency issue relates to the need to constrain expenditure and reduce budget deficits. It is quite possible that neither of these incentives apply in some PICs.

As Hezel and others have pointed out, a number of PICs accept that there is little prospect for ever becoming economically competitive or self-sufficient. They do not aspire to attract substantial foreign direct investment or to compete in the export of goods and services. They simply do not have the same economic incentives to improve human capital. In parallel, there are also few incentives to reduce the education wage bill; in some countries the main purpose of the education system is to transfer money to recipients—"workfare." The funding shortfall is met by donor nations and there are no real incentives to economize. Some countries are reconciled to being perpetually dependent on foreign aid, and deficits are not an urgent concern. Therefore, the economic incentives for reform at play in other regions may not exist in some PICs.

Are there any other incentives that might apply to the Pacific region? One plausible incentive is that with a reformed education system, countries could do much better with little or no additional cost. In very simple terms, there is potential for substantial improvements in outcomes with greater efficiency. A nation could have approximately the same number of teachers on the payroll but, by selecting teachers based on their demonstrated productivity rather than through patronage, that nation could have much better learning outcomes. The social costs of a transformed system would be low; the political costs, however, might be high. The benefits would take the form of a public good; students would leave school with higher levels of literacy and numeracy. This would undoubtedly be beneficial to urban dwellers and migrants and probably would have positive impacts in rural communities where most residents engage in subsistence agriculture. Of course, the problem with public goods is that, unlike patronage, there is a weaker basis for demanding reciprocity. Unless there is strong social demand for public goods, there is no payoff to officials who provide them. Under the existing system, wasteful and inefficient patronage is financed at the cost of reduced learning. In some ways, maintaining the status quo is the functional equivalent of depleting a national trust fund to buy short-term political support. Of course, this problem is not unique to PICs; it is inherent in political processes worldwide.

> **The social costs of a transformed system would be low; the political costs, however, might be high.**

Feasibility

In some countries, the political system depends on the existing patronage system. The big men deliver the goodies and, in return, they are able to garner the votes. Since the education system is the largest source of public employment, there is the risk that dismantling the patronage system would undermine the political advantage of the party and officials in power. Also, teachers constitute a large and often well-organized interest group; in some countries, teachers are used as election monitors. Clearly, many teachers would have a stake in opposing reform, especially if jobs were on the line. There certainly is evidence of a strong constituency for patronage, in general. Many households share the benefits of teachers' salaries. Therefore, one must consider whether there would be sufficient public support for improved education to offset vested interests in the status quo. Also, as the head of the party in power, could a national leader convince his or her colleagues to relinquish these advantages? My guess is that, if the transition were abrupt and disruptive, the answer would be "no." Reform might be feasible if it were managed to minimize disruption.

Managing the process

This suggests that reform would need to be a slow process, based on persuasive evidence that, in the long term, benefits would greatly outweigh costs. I would argue that the first step in a transition process is the *objective* and *independent* collection and analysis of the facts. This would be an independent and data-driven assessment of the key characteristics of the system: access, quality, equity, efficiency, and sustainability. Questions might include the following: How is the national system doing compared to other countries? Has quality been improving, declining, or stagnating? How are individual schools performing relative to each another? What are the differences between geographic regions, ethnic groups, and gender? Which teachers produce significant learning gains and which do not? What are the correlates of teacher effectiveness? What are the unit costs at each institution and how do they differ by levels of the system? How cost effective are different institutions and what factors explain differences? Are public funds allocated equitably, and what share of total expenditure (over the entire education cycle, including tertiary and scholarships) goes to different socioeconomic groups? What are the labor-market outcomes of graduates? Who emigrates and why? What is the experience of emigrants and what are their perceptions of the quality of the education they received at home?

> The first step in a transition process is the objective and independent collection and analysis of the facts.

In the interest of independence and objectivity, I suggest that the mandate for fact-finding be given to individuals in-country, but from *outside* the education establishment. Analysts in central ministries, such as finance or economic planning, should have the skills required. In all probability, additional primary data will be required to answer some of these questions and the unit or group charged with fact finding should have sufficient resources and time for data collection. I also believe that it would be important to limit the mandate to reporting facts; the analysts should not be asked to provide recommendations on reform or to assess the performance of the institutions. The output would simply be an independent review of the current situation, with special emphasis on individual student learning. Yet, there should be a clear requirement for quantified empirical evidence to support all findings.

I am not suggesting another report. As discussed earlier, reports generally end up on a shelf, covered with dust. What is needed is an independent monitoring and assessment *process*—a system for objective assessment and feedback to the national leader, describing where money is going and whether the country is getting value for money. I am definitely not suggesting a white paper. The white-paper process often generates an elaborate shopping list of expensive and unnecessary appendages to the education system. As noted earlier, the problem is not insufficient resources; it is lack if incentives and inefficiency.

> **The mandate for fact-finding should be given to individuals in-country, but from *outside* the education establishment.**

If several PIC leaders decided to undertake parallel education assessments, there would be advantages to providing opportunities for collaboration and information sharing. Analysts could meet periodically to share ideas on methodology and possibly collaborate in developing common instruments. It might be possible to obtain additional training and technical assistance for the group, but I believe that it would be a serious error to outsource the activity to a donor organization or consultants.

Once data have been collected and analyses completed, the next step would be to hold internal meetings with key political and government officials to review findings and determine whether there is consensus regarding the need for reform. If, based on objective evidence, there is agreement that fundamental reform makes sense, senior officials could develop a collaborative strategy for change.

Given that the existing patronage system is so integral to the social and economic fabric of some PICs, it would be important to build national support for change. Information collected during the initial assessment phase could provide the basis for a public-awareness campaign. If there was broad political support for reform, including endorsement by opposition parliamentarians, public support could probably be mobilized. If proposed reforms included a transition to greater community control through decentralization, this might also generate more grassroots support.

Movements toward reform and teacher accountability have met resistance from teachers and teacher unions in most countries. It would be surprising if this were not the case. Through dialogue based on clear objective evidence, it has been possible to slowly build support and gain concessions from teacher unions. If there are transparent criteria for teacher assessment and consensus on the need to improve learning outcomes, change is possible.

There would be substantial one-time costs associated with the retrenchment of ineffective teachers. It would be important to have a generous retrenchment package for employees who were terminated and replaced, possibly linked to retraining and/or opportunities to start small businesses. My guess is that if a plan for genuine and transparent reform were developed, donor agencies would be willing to meet some or all of the transition costs. There are examples of successful strategies for teacher retrenchment; many of these come from countries facing rapid declines in the student population, such as Bulgaria, Latvia, Romania, and Moldova. The World Bank has been involved in a number of these initiatives.

Realistically, there would be some well-connected but ineffective teachers who would have to be offered alternative public employment. This is an ongoing problem in all government bureaucracies. Every government creates commissions or special bodies to accommodate that problem. If, for whatever reason, some people do need to be on the public payroll, they should be in positions where they do no harm. If someone sits in a government office doing nothing, at least he or she is doing no harm. It is unconscionable to deprive children of the opportunity to learn because somebody's nephew needs a job.

> It is unconscionable to deprive children of the opportunity to learn because somebody's nephew needs a job.

To summarize, the core element of the reform I suggest would be moving to a system where *demonstrating* the ability to produce learning gains in children (value added) would be a precondition for continued employment as a teacher. This argument is premised on two assumptions. The first assumption is that there are other people in PICs who are willing and able to be effective teachers or that competent and motivated candidates could be identified and trained. The second assumption is that there are individuals or organizations that can effectively manage schools and implement accountability. It would be possible to test these assumptions through phased implementation of reforms, with rigorous assessment of student outcomes. International evidence suggests that new teachers probably do not need a formal teaching qualification to do the job.

The unfortunate state of education in many PICs reflects decades of bad policies and decisions on the part of former colonial powers, well-intentioned donor organizations, and political leaders. There is little to be gained by assigning blame, but there is almost no prospect for improvement unless the existing problems are openly acknowledged.

My own assessment is that the existing education systems in many PICs are not the best they can be. I believe that Pacific Island leaders can bring about substantial reform and improvement, if there is political will.

References

Abbott, D., and S. Pollard. 2004. *Hardship and Poverty in the Pacific.* Manila: Asian Development Bank.

ADB. See Asian Development Bank.

Asian Development Bank. 2007. *Support for Results-Based Management in the Pacific.* Regional Technical Assistance Report, Project Number 38637, October 2007. Manila: Asian Development Bank. http://www.adb.org/Documents/TARs/REG/38637-REG-TAR.pdf.

_____. 2009. *Good Practice in Cost Sharing and Financing in Education.* Manila: Asian Development Bank.

_____. 2010. *Transparency to the People Using Stakeholder Participation to Support Public Sector Reform in Nauru and the Republic of the Marshall Islands.* Pacific Studies Series. Manila: Asian Development Bank.

_____. 2010a. *MDG Priorities in Asia and the Pacific: Asia-Pacific MDG Report 2010/11.* Manila: Asian Development Bank.

Asadullah, M.N. 2005. "The Effect of Class Size on Student Achievement: Evidence From Bangladesh." *Applied Economics Letters* 12 (4): 217–221.

Asia South Pacific Association for Basic and Adult Education. 2011. *ODA for Education in Asia and the Pacific.* Mumbai: Asia South Pacific Association for Basic and Adult Education.

ASPBAE. *See* Asia South Pacific Association for Basic and Adult Education.

ASPEW. *See* Asia-South Pacific Education Watch.

Associated Press. 2009. "Education chief: Overhaul Teacher Training." October 21.

Asia-South Pacific Education Watch. 2007. *Papua New Guinea: Summary Report Survey of Education Experience.* Mumbai: Asian-South Pacific Education Watch.

AusAID. *See* Australian Agency for International Development.

Australian Agency for International Development. 2007. *Better Education: A Policy for Development Assistance in Education.* Canberra: Australian Agency for International Development.

_____. 2009. *Tracking Development and Governance in the Pacific.* Canberra: Australian Agency for International Development.

_____. 2010. *Annual Thematic Performance Report 2009: Education.* Canberra: Australian Agency for International Development.

_____. 2011. http://www.ausaid.gov.au/keyaid/education.cfm.

_____. 2011a. *Measuring the Quality of Education.* http://www.ausaid.gov.au/keyaid/edu_quality.cfm.

Borland, M.V., R.M. Howsen, and M.W. Trawick. 2005. "An Investigation of the Effect of Class Size on Student Academic Achievement." *Education Economics* 13 (1): 73–83.

Bressoux, P., F. Kramarz, and C. Prost. 2009. "Teachers' Training, Class Size and Students' Outcomes: Learning From Administrative Forecasting Mistakes." *Economic Journal* 119 (536): 540–561.

Brown, R., and E. Jimenez. 2008. "Estimating the Net Effects of Migration and Remittances on Poverty and Inequality: Comparison of Fiji and Tonga." *Journal of International Development* 20: 547–571.

Bruns, B., D. Filmer, and H. Patrinos. 2011. *Making Schools Work: New Evidence on Accountability Reforms.* Washington: World Bank.

Carey, K., and R. Manwaring. 2011. *Growth Models and Accountability: A Recipe for Remaking ESEA.* Education Sector Reports. Washington: Education Sector. http://www.educationsector.org/sites/default/files/publications/GrowthModelsAndAccountability_Release%20.pdf.

Chaudhury, N., J.S. Hammer, M. Kremer, K. Muralidharan, and F.H. Rogers. 2006. "Missing in Action: Teacher and Health Worker Absence in Developing Countries." *Journal of Economic Perspectives,* 20 (1): 91–116.

Chutaro, E., and H. Heine. 2003. "A Double-Edged Sword: A Study of the Impact of External Educational Aid to the Republic of the Marshall Islands." Paper presented at the Rethinking Educational Aid in the Pacific Conference, Nadi, Fiji, October 20–22.

Corak, M., and D. Lauzon. 2009. "Differences in the Distribution of High School Achievement: The Role of Class-Size and Time-In-Term." *Economics of Education Review,* 28 (2): 189–198.

Ding, W., and S. Lehrer. 2005. "Class Size and Student Achievement: Experimental Estimates of Who Benefits and Who Loses from Reductions." Queen's Economics Working Paper No. 1046, Department of Economics, Queen's University, Kingston, Ontario, Canada. http://www.econ.queensu.ca/working_papers/papers/qed_wp_1046.pdf. Retrieved from www.csa.com (1046; 0842088).

Duncan, R., ed. 2010. *The Political Economy of Economic Reform in the Pacific.* Manila: Asian Development Bank.

Eremae, O. 2005. "Solomons Shoulder Tuition for Ministers' Kids." *Solomon Star* (Honiara, Solomon Islands), October 13.

Feeny, S. and M. Rogers. 2008. "Policy Arena: Public Sector Efficiency, Foreign Aid and Small Island Developing States." *Journal of International Development* 20: 526–546.

Fehrler, S., Michaelowa, K., and Wechtler, A. 2009. "The Effectiveness of Inputs in Primary Education: Insights From Recent Student Surveys for Sub-Saharan Africa." *Journal of Development Studies* 45 (9): 1545–1578.

Filmer, D. 2010. *Education Attainment and Enrollment Around the World: An International Database.* Washington: The World Bank. htpp:/econ.worldbank.org/projects/edattain.

Funkhouser, E. 2009. "The Effect of Kindergarten Classroom Size Reduction on Second Grade Student Achievement: Evidence From California." *Economics of Education Review* 28 (3): 403–414.

Gordon, R., T. Kane, and D. Staiger. 2006. "Identifying Effective Teachers Using Performance on the Job." The Hamilton Project, discussion paper. Washington: Brookings Institution.

Hanushek, E. 2010. "The Economic Value of Higher Teacher Quality." National Bureau of Economic Research Working Paper No. 16606, National Bureau of Economic Research: Cambridge, MA.

Hanushek, E. and L. Woessmann. 2008. "The Role of Cognitive Skills in Economic Development." *Journal of Economic Literature*, 46 (3): 607–68.

Hart, T. 2009. "Guam Keeps Wary Eye On Hawai'i Cuts: Micronesians Could Turn to Guam for Health Care." *Pacific Daily News* (Hagatna, Guam), August 31.

———. 2011. "Hawai'i's Costs of Federal Migration Treaty Rise." *Garden Island* (Lihue, Hawai'i), August 12.

Hayward-Jones, J. 2008. *Beyond Good Governance: Shifting the Paradigm for Australian Aid to the Pacific Islands Region.* Policy Brief. Sydney: Lowy Institute for International Policy.

Hezel, F. 2001. "Islands of Excellence." *Micronesian Counselor* 34: April. http://www.micsem.org/pubs/counselor/frames/islandsfr.htm.

———. 2006. *Is That the Best You Can Do? A Tale of Two Micronesian Economies.* Pacific Islands Policy 1. Honolulu: East-West Center, Pacific Islands Development Program.

Hughes, H. 2002. Submission to Senate Foreign Affairs, Defense and Trade References Committee. Canberra: March, 2002.

Johnson, G. 2004. "Most Marshall Islands Teachers Flunk Tests." *Marianas Variety* (Majuro), April 5.

———. 2005. "Cohen: Pacific Needs to Push Education." *Marianas Variety* (Majuro), July 18.

———. 2011. "Teacher Vacancies Stymie Marshalls Education: Jobs Unfilled For Months." *Marianas Variety* (Majuro), April 25.

Kane, T., J. Rockoff, and D. Staiger. 2008. "What Does Certification Tell Us About Teacher Effectiveness? Evidence from New York City." *Economics of Education Review* 27: 615–631.

Lawson, M. 2010. *Foreign Aid: International Donor Coordination of Development Assistance.* Washington: Congressional Research Service. http://fpc.state.gog/document/organization/142758.pdf.

Leuven, E., H. Oosterbeek, and M. Ronning. 2008. "Quasi-Experimental Estimates of the Effect of Class Size on Achievement in Norway." *Scandinavian Journal of Economics*, 110 (4): 663–693.

Levine, A. 2006. *Educating School Teachers*. Washington: The Education Schools Project.

Levine, V. 2009. *Review of Education Sector Management in Chuuck*. Consultant report. Manila: Asian Development Bank.

Lewis, S. 2011. "Foreign Advisors Raking in Missions." *Daily Telegraph* (Surry Hills, NSW, Australia), July 1.

_____. 2011a. "Foreign Aid Millionaires: The Consultants Getting Rich on Others,' Misfortune." *Advertiser* (Adelaide, SA, Australia), July 1. Lewis, S. and N. Christensen. 2010. "Foreign Aid Millions Lost, Review Finds." *Mercury* (Hobart, Tasmania, Australia), May 24.

Limtiaco, S. 2003. "Public Education Raises Concern on Guam." Hagatna: *Pacific Daily News* (Hagatna, Guam), September 11.

Lindahl, M. 2005. "Home Versus School Learning: A New Approach to Estimating the Effect of Class Size on Achievement." *Scandinavian Journal of Economics*, 107 (2), 375–394.

Marshall Islands Journal (Majuro). 2001. "Why Can't Marshall Islands Education Be More Like Palau's?" August 17.

Matangi (Nukuʻalofa, Tonga). 2010. "Media Encouraged to Better Report on Education." March 25.

McKee, G.J., S.G. Rivkin, and K.R.E. Sims. 2010. "Disruption, Achievement and the Heterogeneous Benefits of Smaller Classes." *National Bureau of Economic Research Working Paper No. 15812*. National Bureau of Economic Research: Cambridge, MA. http://www.nber.org/papers/w15812.pdf.

Michaelowa, K., and E. Wittmann. 2007. "The Cost, Satisfaction, and Achievement of Primary Education: Evidence from Francophone Sub-Saharan Africa." *Journal of Developing Areas* 41 (1): 51–78.

Naidu, S., and S. Prasad. 2002. "Pacific Education Issues 'Old Wine In New Bottle,': Thaman." *Wansolwara Online* (University of the South Pacific), April 27.

National (Port Moresby). 2004. "PNG Educators Assess School System," July 13.

_____. 2007. "PNG Province Gives Up on Free Education Offering," November 13.

_____. 2010. "A Double Standard for PBG Public Officials," March 3.

Northern Territory News (Darwin, NT, Australia). 2010. "Our Foreign Aid Program Under Siege for 'Wasteful' Use of Money and Resources." May 24.

Pacific Daily News (Hagatna, Guam). 2006. "Politics Trumps Performance in Guam School System." June 15.

_____. 2011. "Guam Education Must Stop Ignoring Financial Woes." June 20.

_____. 2011a. "Guam School Budget Request Unrealistic." January 26.

Pacific Islands Forum Secretariat. 2006. *Education Ministers Meeting: Proposal on a Pacific Programme for the Fast Track Initiative for Education for All.* Nadi: Pacific Islands Forum Secretariat, September, 2006.

_____. 2009. Review of the Forum Basic Education Action Plan (FBEAP). Suva: Pacific Islands Forum Secretariat, January.

_____. 2009a. "Forum Education Ministers Discuss Regional Framework for Education." Press release. March 25.

_____. 2010. "Literacy and Numeracy in FICs." *Solomon Times Online* (Honiara, Solomon Islands). http://www.solomontimes.com/news.aspx?nwID=5446.

PIFS. *See* Pacific Islands Forum Secretariat.

PINA Nius Online (Wellington, New Zealand). 2001. "Millions Of Pacific Education Aid Money Misspent, Says Report." April 30.

Post Courier (Port Moresby). 2010. "PNG Island Provinces Fall Behind In Education." April 19.

_____. 2010a. "PNG Makes Major Investment in Education." November 18.

Psacharopolous, G., and H. Patrinos. 2002. "Returns to Investment in Education: A Further Update." World Bank Policy Research Working Paper No. 2881, Washington: World Bank. September.

Radio New Zealand International. 2010. "Pacific Islanders Lag in New Zealand Schools." June 17, 2010.

Rivkin, S.G., E.A. Hanushek, and J.F. Kain. 2005. "Teachers, Schools, and Academic Achievement." *Econometrica*, 73 (2): 417–458.

Rockoff, J. 2009. "Field Experiments in Class Size from the Early Twentieth Century." *Journal of Economic Perspectives*, 23 (4): 211–230.

Rowa, A. 2007. "High Truancy, Low Success Plague Marshalls Schools." *Yokwe Online* (Majuro), April 30.

Sanga, K. 2003. "A Context-Sensitive Approach to Educational Aid." *Directions: Journal of Educational Studies* 25 (1, 2).

Schwarz, A. 2011. "Union Chief Faults School Reform From 'On High.'" *New York Times*. http://www.nytimes.com/2011/07/12/us/12aft.html?_r=1&hpw.

Secretariat of the Pacific Community. 2011. *Literacy and Numeracy Project Updates.* Suva: Secretariat of the Pacific Community, Vol. 1, April.

Solomon Star (Honiara, Solomon Islands). 2006. "Untrained Teachers Major Concern in Solomons." January 9.

South Pacific Board for Educational Assessment. 2011. http://www.spbea.org.fj/.

SPBEA. *See* South Pacific Board for Educational Assessment.

SPC. *See* Secretariat of the Pacific Community.

Tang, T., and J. Williams. 2000. "Misalignment of Learning Contexts: An Explanation of the Chinese Learner Paradox." School of Economics and Finance, Queensland University of Technology, School of Economics and Finance Discussion Papers and Working Papers Series. http://www.bus.qut.edu.au/faculty/schools/economics/documents/discussionPapers/2000/Tang_Williams_79.pdf.

Urquiola, M. 2006. "Identifying Class Size Effects in Developing Countries: Evidence from Rural Bolivia." *Review of Economics and Statistics* 88 (1): 171–177.

Withers, G. n.d. "The Pacific Islands Literacy Levels: Some Implications for Learning and Teaching." Mimeo.

World Bank. 2006. *Opportunities to Improve Social Services: Human Development in the Pacific Islands*. Washington, DC: Human Development Sector Unit, East Asia and Pacific Region, World Bank.

_____. 2007. *Human Development in the Pacific Islands: Opportunities to Improve Education Sector Performance*. Summary Report 38865. Washington, DC: World Bank.

_____. 2010. *Malaysia Economic Monitor: Growth Through Innovation*. Washington, DC: World Bank.

_____. 2011. Data downloaded in September. http://data.worldbank.org/indicator/DT.ODA.ODAT.PC.ZS.

_____. 2011a. *Learning for All: Investing in People's Knowledge and Skills to Promote Development*. World Bank Group Education Strategy 2020. Washington: The International Bank for Reconstruction and Development/The World Bank. http://siteresources.worldbank.org/EDUCATION/Resources/ESSU/Education_Strategy_4_12_2011.pdf.

_____. 2011b. *World Development Indicators: Statistics for Small States: A Supplement to the World Development Indicators*.

Woessmann, L. 2005. "Educational Production in Europe." *Economic Policy* 43: 445–493.

Xinhua News Agency. 2011. "Australia, New Zealand Step Up Aid for Basic Education in Pacific." September 7.

Yeh, S.S., and J. Ritter. 2009. "The Cost-Effectiveness of Replacing the Bottom Quartile of Novice Teachers Through Value-Added Teacher Assessment." *Journal of Education Finance*, 34 (4): 426–451.

Young, A. 2011. "Horror Pacific Island Education Stats." *New Zealand Herald* (Auckland), September 5.

_____. 2011a. "McCully Wants More Bang for Pacific Education Aid Bucks." *New Zealand Herald*. September 6.

The Author

Victor Levine has been working in international development for over 40 years. Following his US Peace Corps experience at a secondary school in Afghanistan, he completed a PhD in education economics at Columbia University in New York. He has taught education economics at Penn State University and the University of Zimbabwe. Currently, Levine is a nonresident fellow with the Pacific Islands Development Program at the East-West Center.

Levine spent most of his non-academic career working on education issues in developing countries. He spent 16 years in Africa and moved to Polynesia in 2001, focusing primarily on Asia Pacific education during the past decade. Levine is now an independent consultant, based on the island of Kauaʻi, in Hawaiʻi. He has extensive experience as a technical adviser to national governments and to a range of multilateral and bilateral donor agencies, foundations, and nongovernmental organizations. These include the World Bank, Asian Development Bank, and United States Agency for International Development.

Levine is the coauthor of *Nurturing Advanced Technology Enterprises: Emerging Issues in State and Local Economic Development Policy* (New York: Praeger, 1986), and he has authored numerous technical reports and journal articles on education economics.

Submissions

Submissions to Pacific Islands Policy may take the form of a proposal or completed manuscript (ideally, 7,000–11,000 words). A proposal should indicate the issue to be analyzed, its policy significance, the contribution the analysis will provide, and the date by which the manuscript will be ready. The series coeditors and editorial board will review the proposal. If a manuscript is considered suitable for the series, it will be peer-reviewed. A curriculum vitae indicating relevant qualifications and publications should accompany submissions. Submissions must be original and not published elsewhere. The author will be asked to assign copyright to the East-West Center.

Notes to Contributors

Manuscripts should be typed, double-spaced, and submitted electronically. The preferred documentation style is for citations to be embedded in the text (*Chicago Manual of Style* author-date system) and accompanied by a complete reference list. Notes should be embedded in the electronic file. All artwork should be camera ready. Send submissions and queries to the series co-editors:

Gerard A. Finin
Resident Co-Director
FininG@EastWestCenter.org

Robert C. Kiste
Adjunct Senior Fellow
KisteR@EastWestCenter.org

Pacific Islands Development Program
East-West Center
1601 East-West Road
Honolulu, Hawai‘i 96848 USA

Tel: 808.944.7745
Fax: 808.944.7670
EastWestCenter.org/pacificislandspolicy

www.ingramcontent.com/pod-product-compliance
Lightning Source LLC
Chambersburg PA
CBHW060353050426
42449CB00011B/2955